AMOK BOOKS
KALEIDOSCOPICS
BOOK 4
"After Dark"

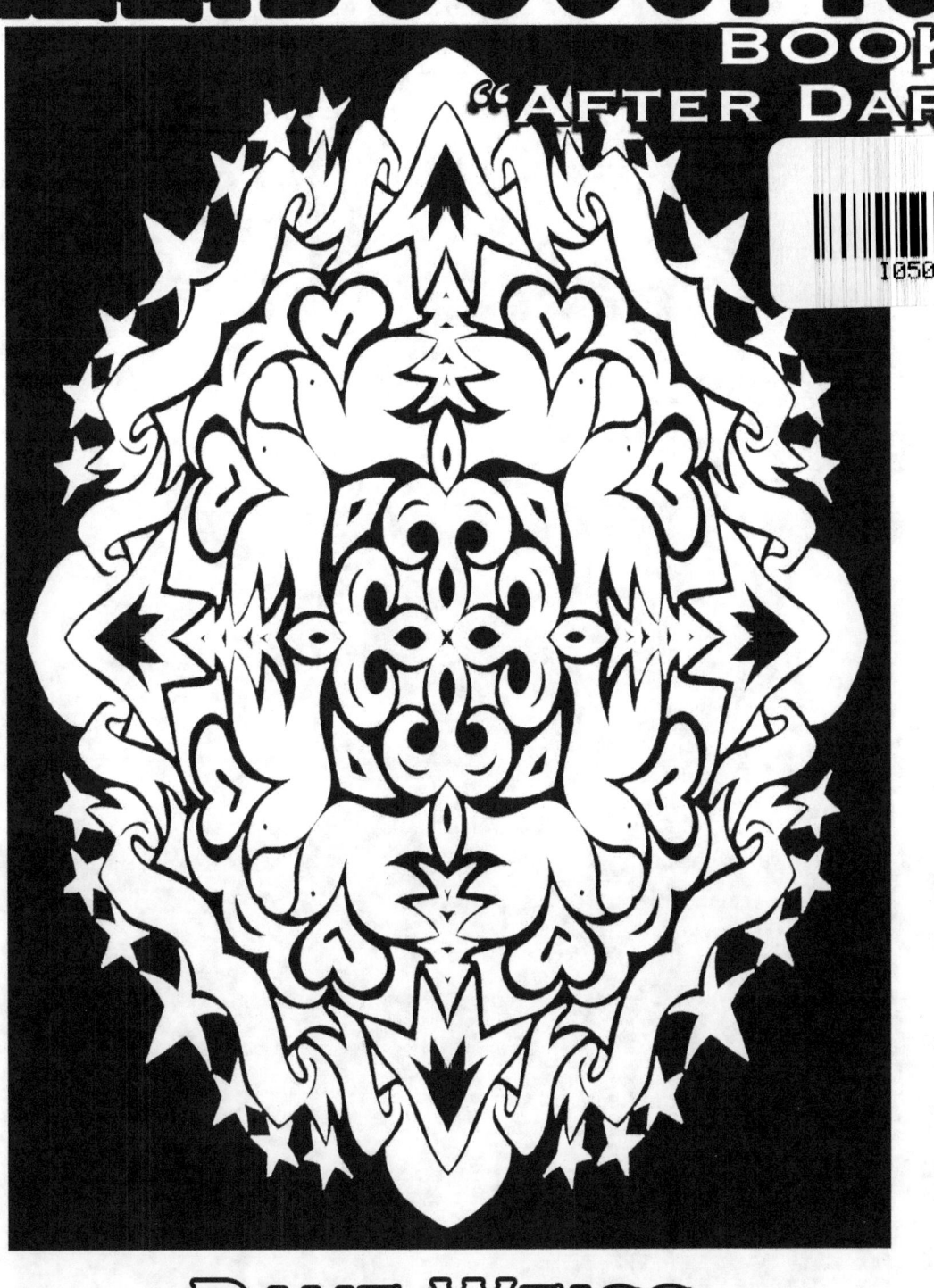

DAVE WEISS
AMOKBOOKS, MOHRSVILLE, PA
DWEISSCREATIVE.COM

Why Kaleidoscopics?

Some people call them Mandalas, but I'm just not comfortable with that. Mandalas are sometimes associated with eastern religious rituals and that's not the direction I'm taking. To me these pieces are a departure from what I usually do. They are created in pieces and cut together into the images you see before you and while I have some idea what the final piece will look like, it is often a very pleasant surprise. It's as if the piece is seen through that favorite childhood toy, a kaleidoscope. For this "After Dark" collection, I decided to add an extra dimension. Creating the images in reverse. Everything coloring space on the final pages was a black area in my drawing. The results were more surprising than ever. I really love these images and hope you will too.

I think of my work on these pages as a kind of artistic jam session—giving my creativity wings and letting it soar. It is my hope that you, the colorist, will do the same. There is no right or wrong way to interpret these, only your way. Have fun with them. Get your materials out and let your creativity take flight. Whether you are coloring just to relax or you're trying to recapture your creativity, know this. You are creative and you are an artist. Pablo Picasso once said, "All children are artists, the problem is to remain one as one grows up."

Welcome back to art. Rermember the point of all of this is to have fun and to reconnect to your inner artist.

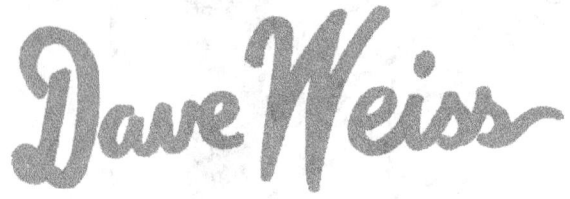

© 2016 by David C Weiss

All rights reserved.
Published Mohrsville, Pennsylvania, by David C. Weiss for AMOK Books. AMOK Books, AMOKArts and A.M.O.K. Arts Ministry Outreach for the Kingdom are trademarks of David C. Weiss

Illustrations by David C. Weiss, AMOKArts.com

ISBN-13: 978-1540545107
ISBN-10: 1540545105

Library of Congress Cataloging-in Publication Data

Weiss, David C,. 1963-
Kaleidoscopics: Book 3, 50 Images to Color by Dave Weiss

ISBN
1. Weiss, David C., 1963- 2. Art
3. Coloring

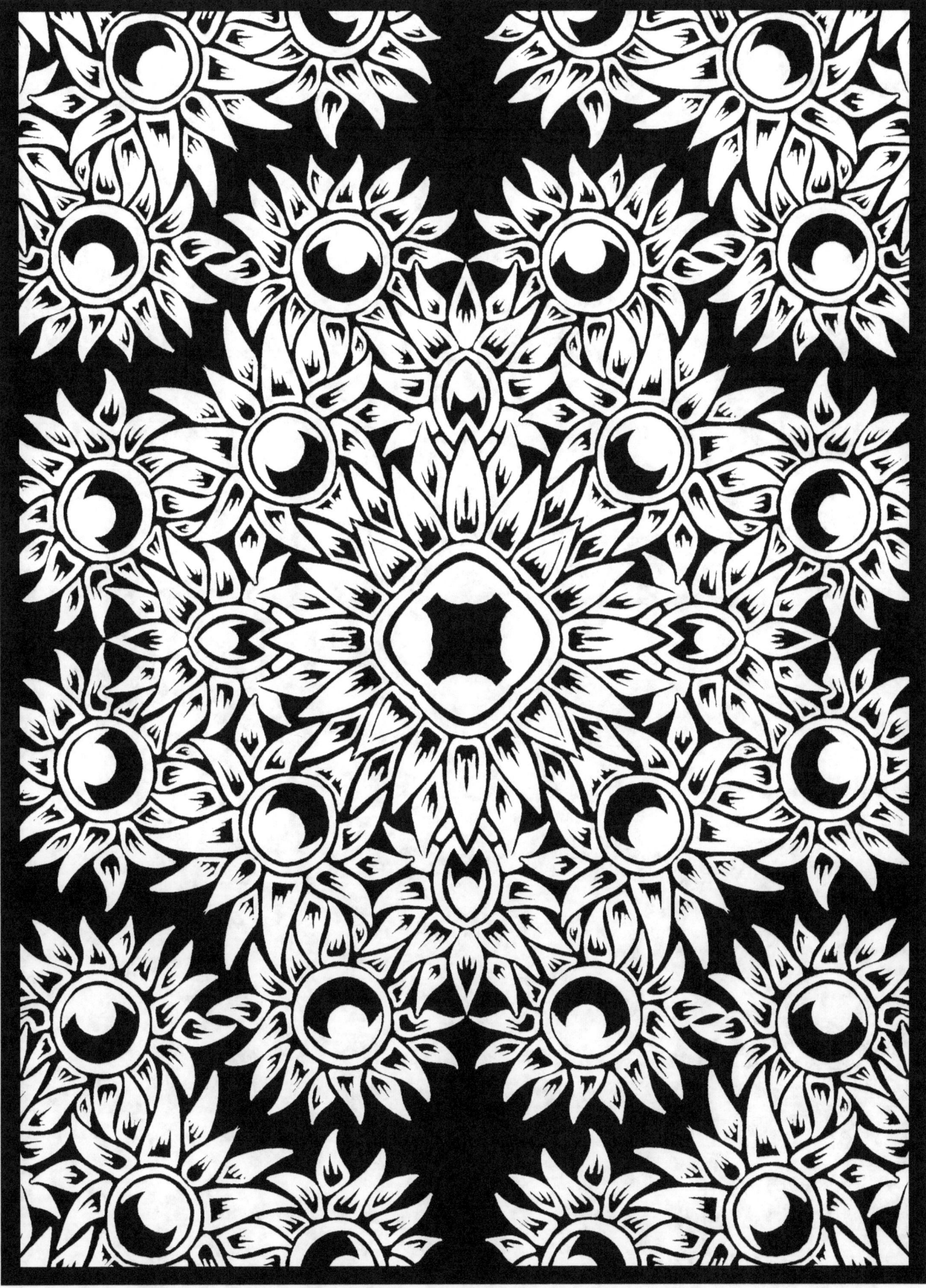

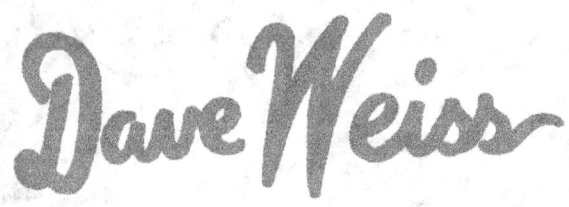

Kaleidoscopics Book 4
"Daisies in the Dark"

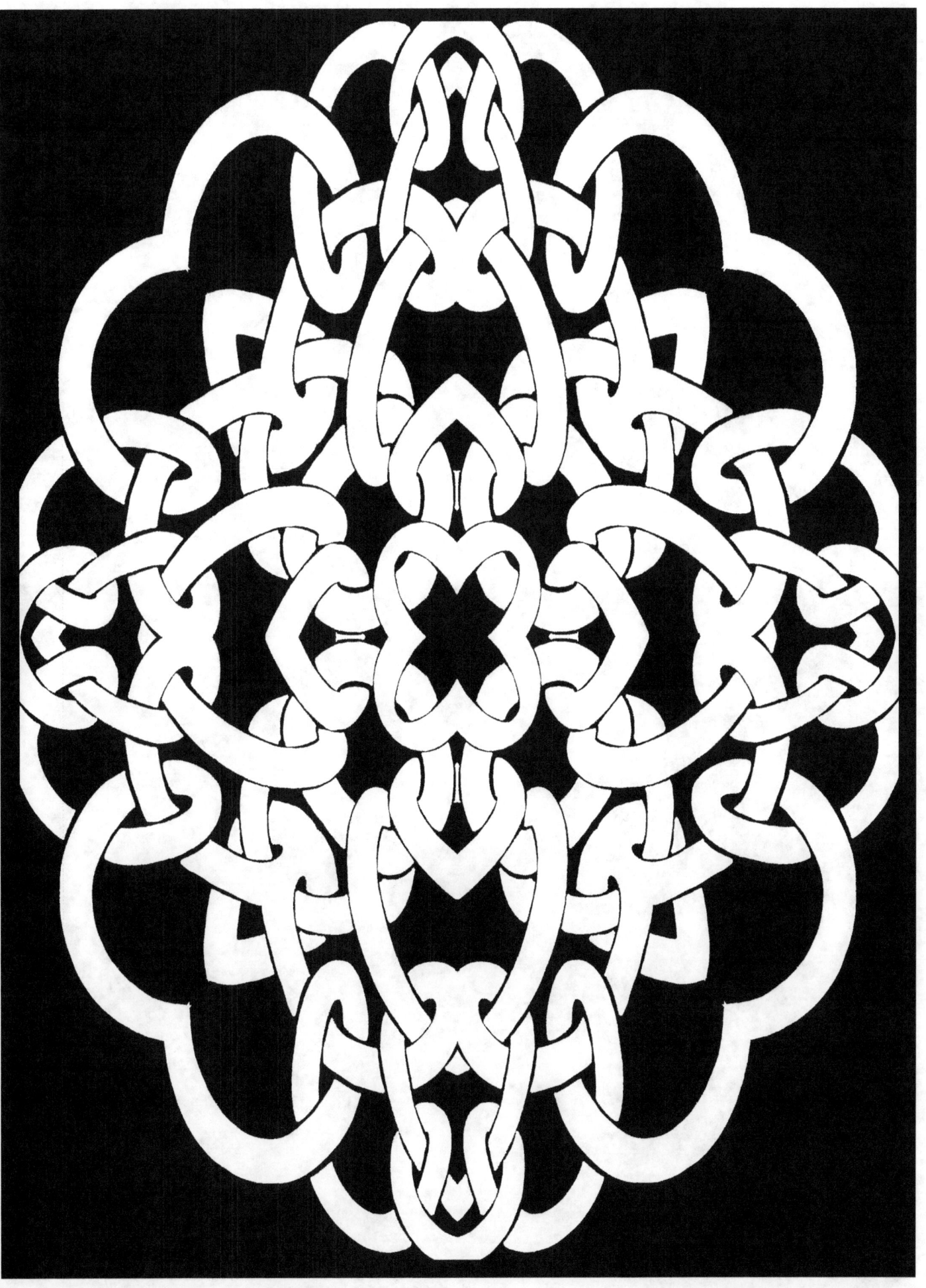

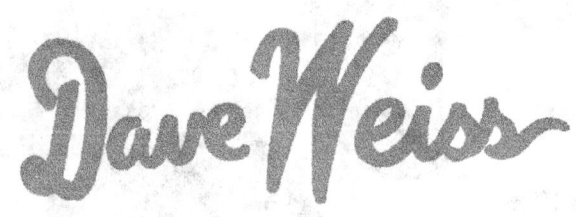

Kaleidoscopics Book 4
"Hearts Entwined"

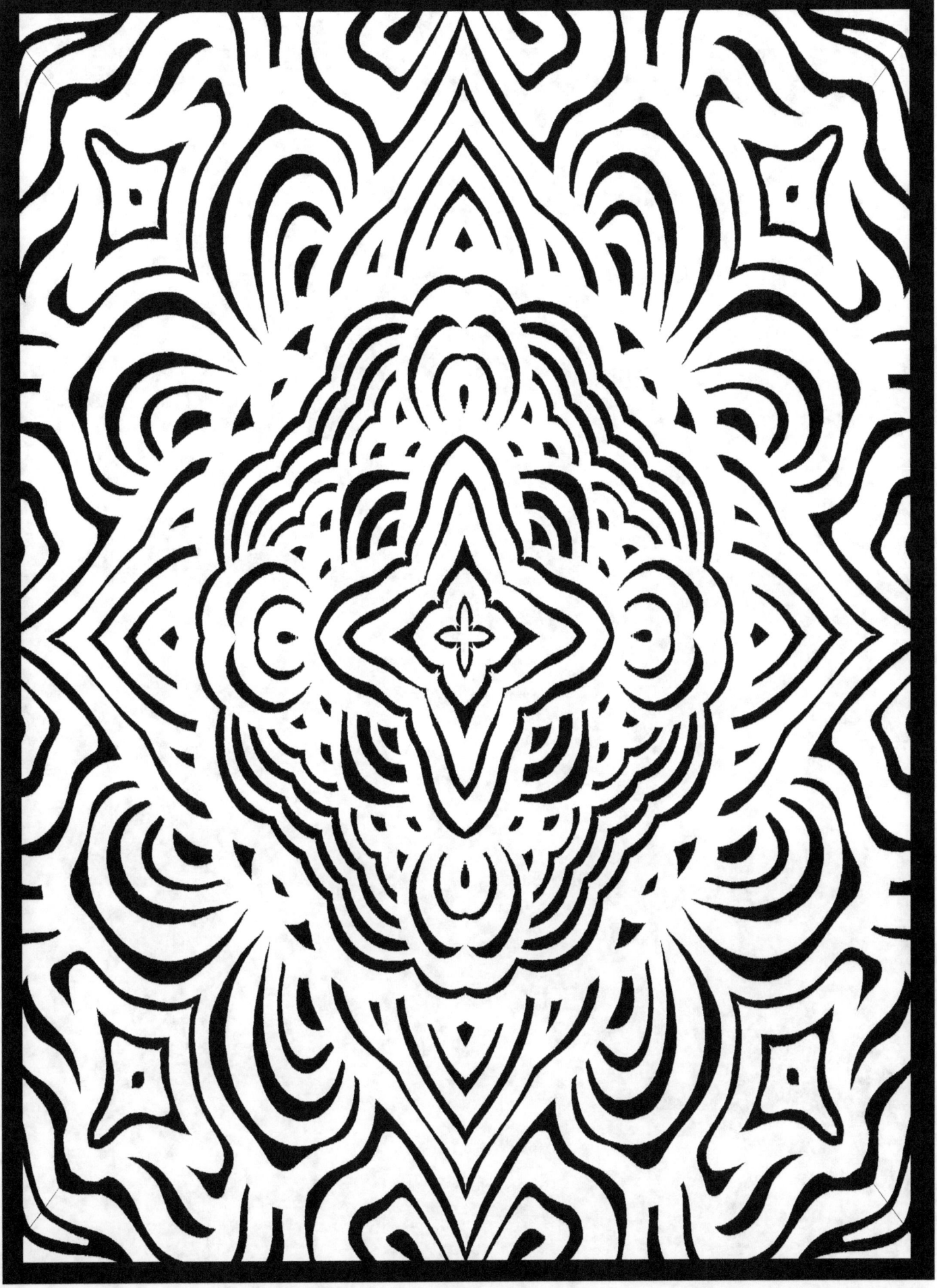

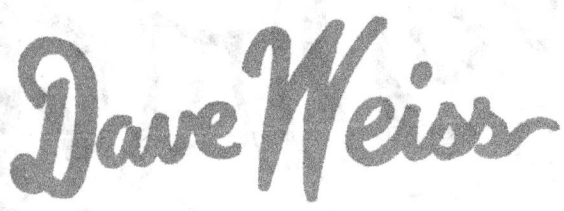

Kaleidoscopics Book 4
"Spacy Lacy"

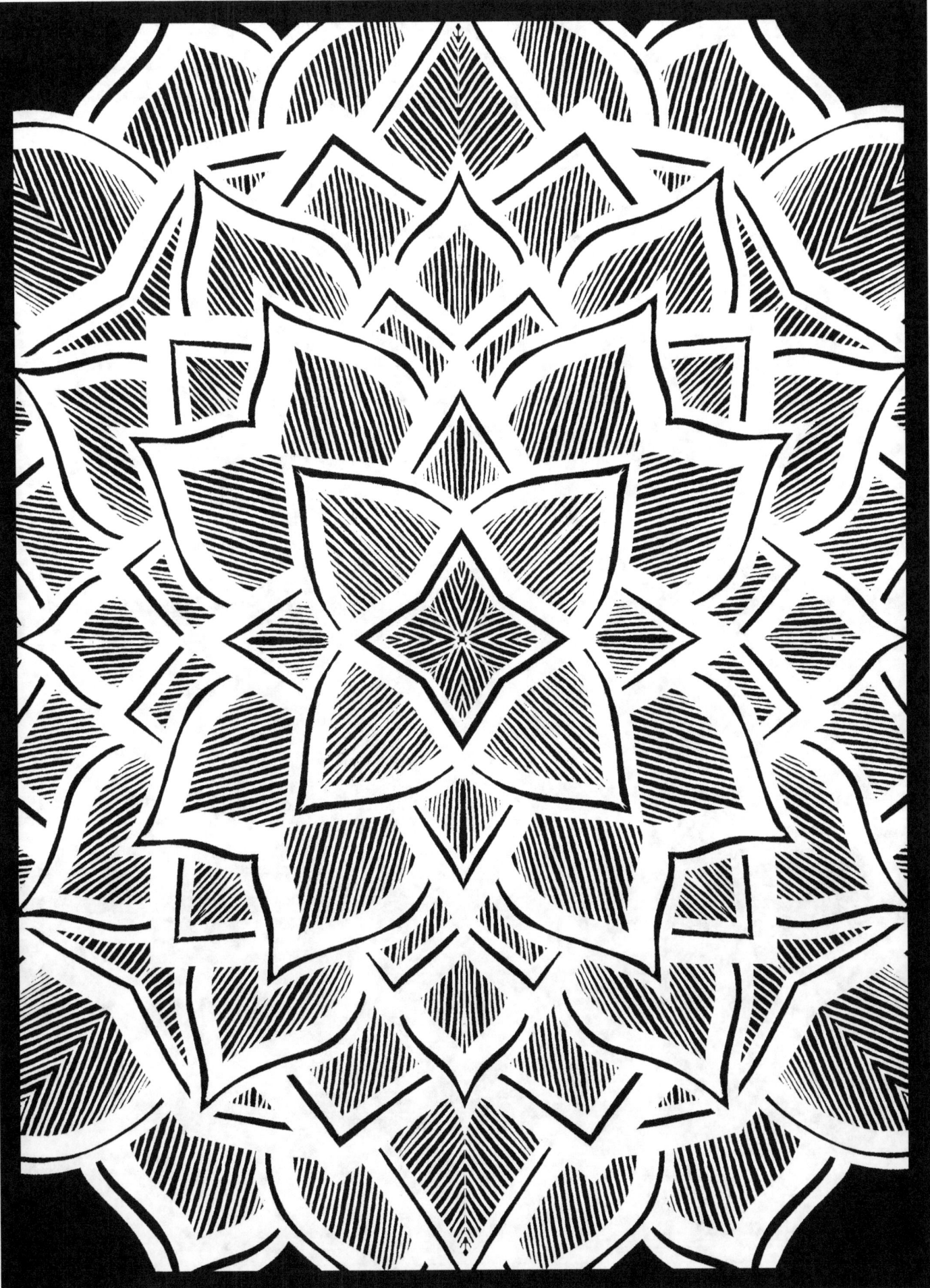

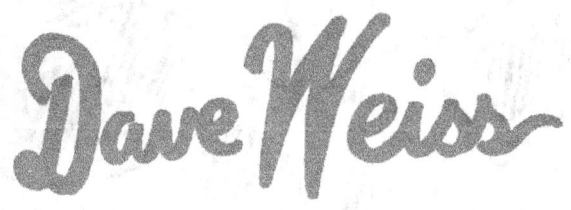

Kaleidoscopics Book 4
"Shady Flower"

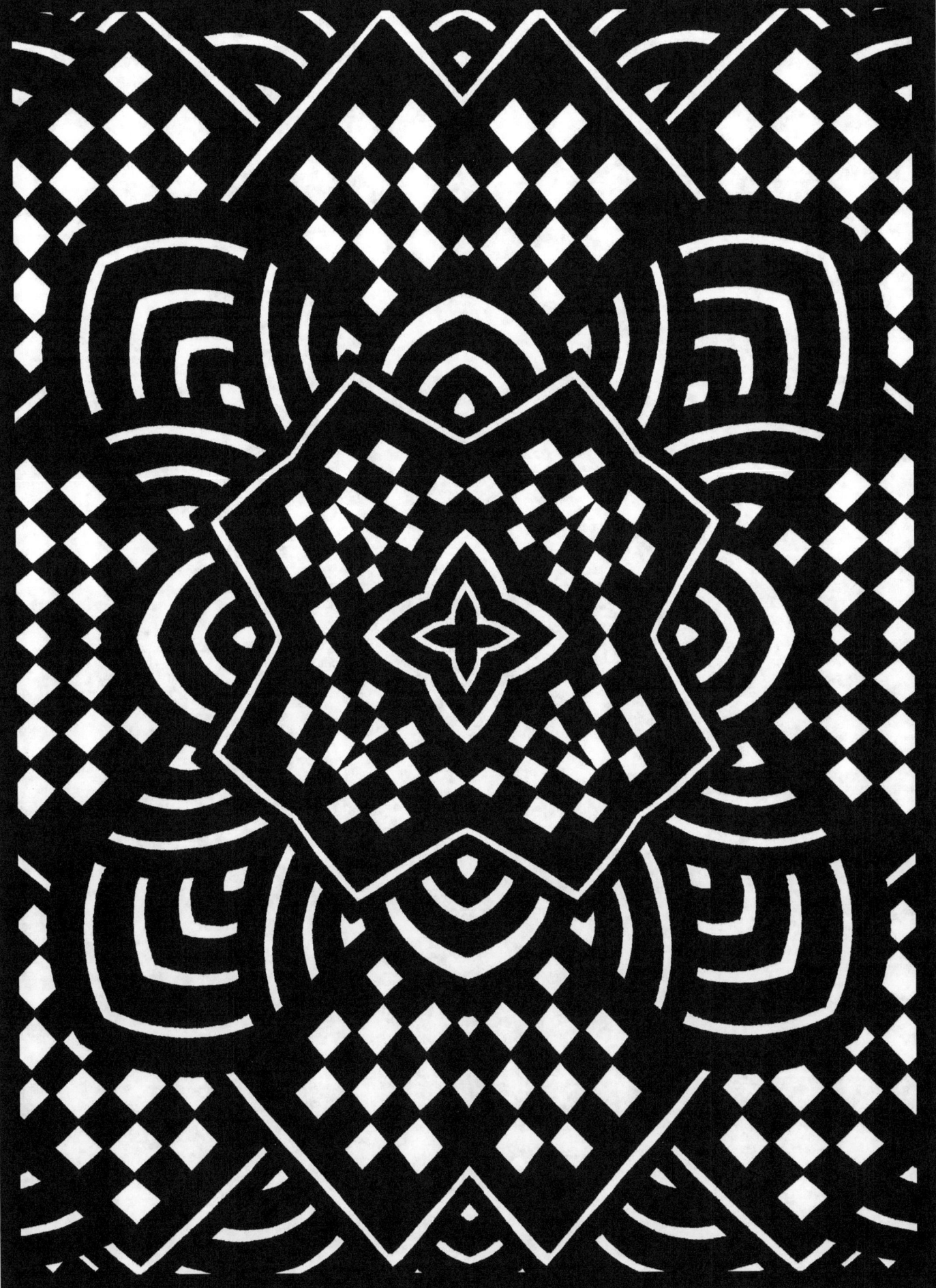

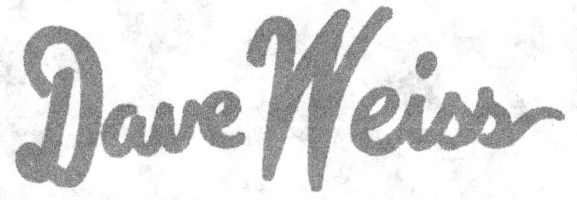

Kaleidoscopics Book 4
"Checkered Past"

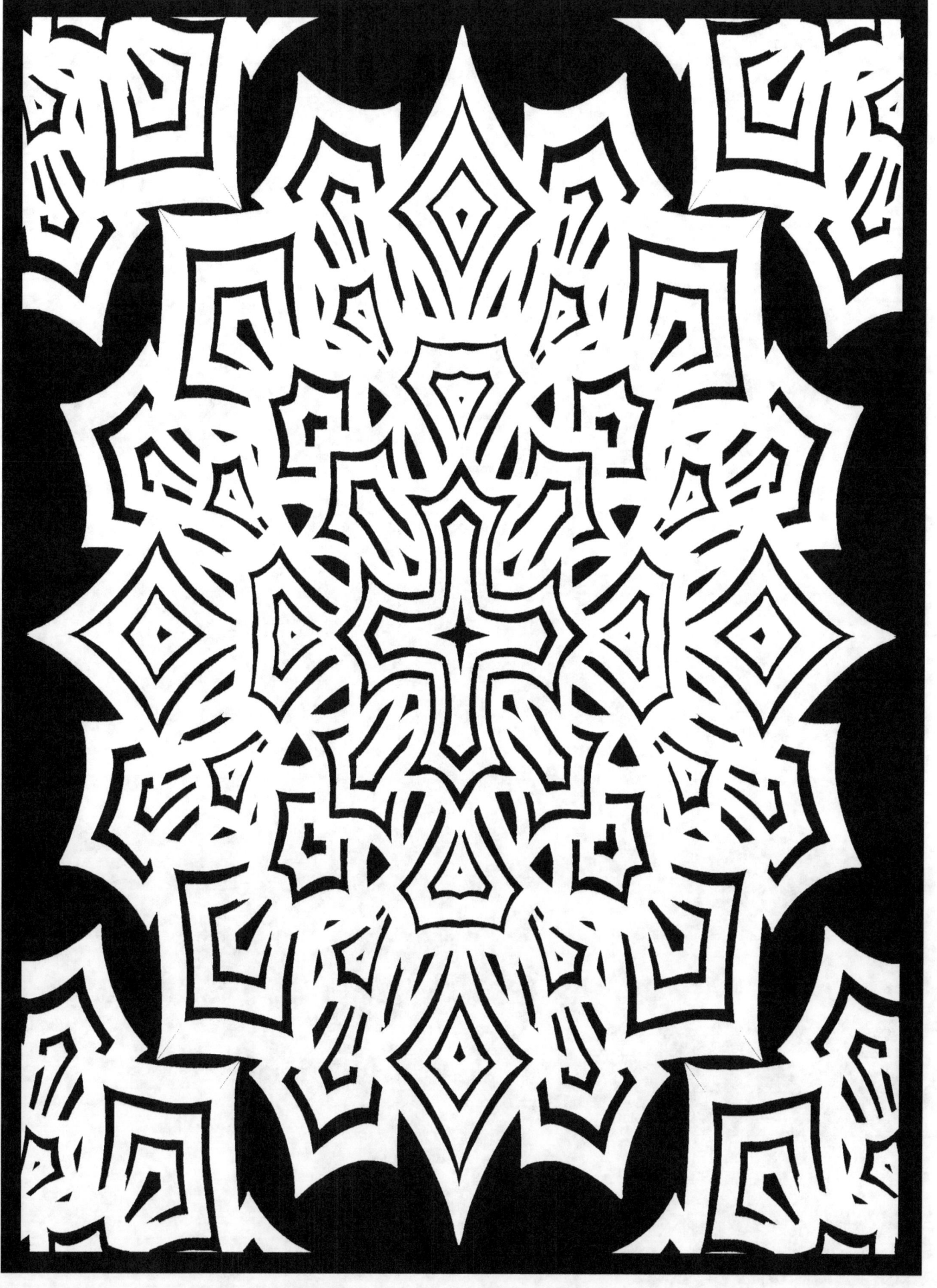

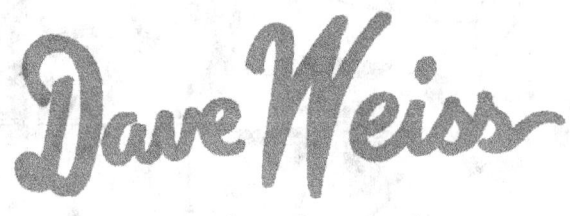

Kaleidoscopics Book 4
"Cross Pointe"

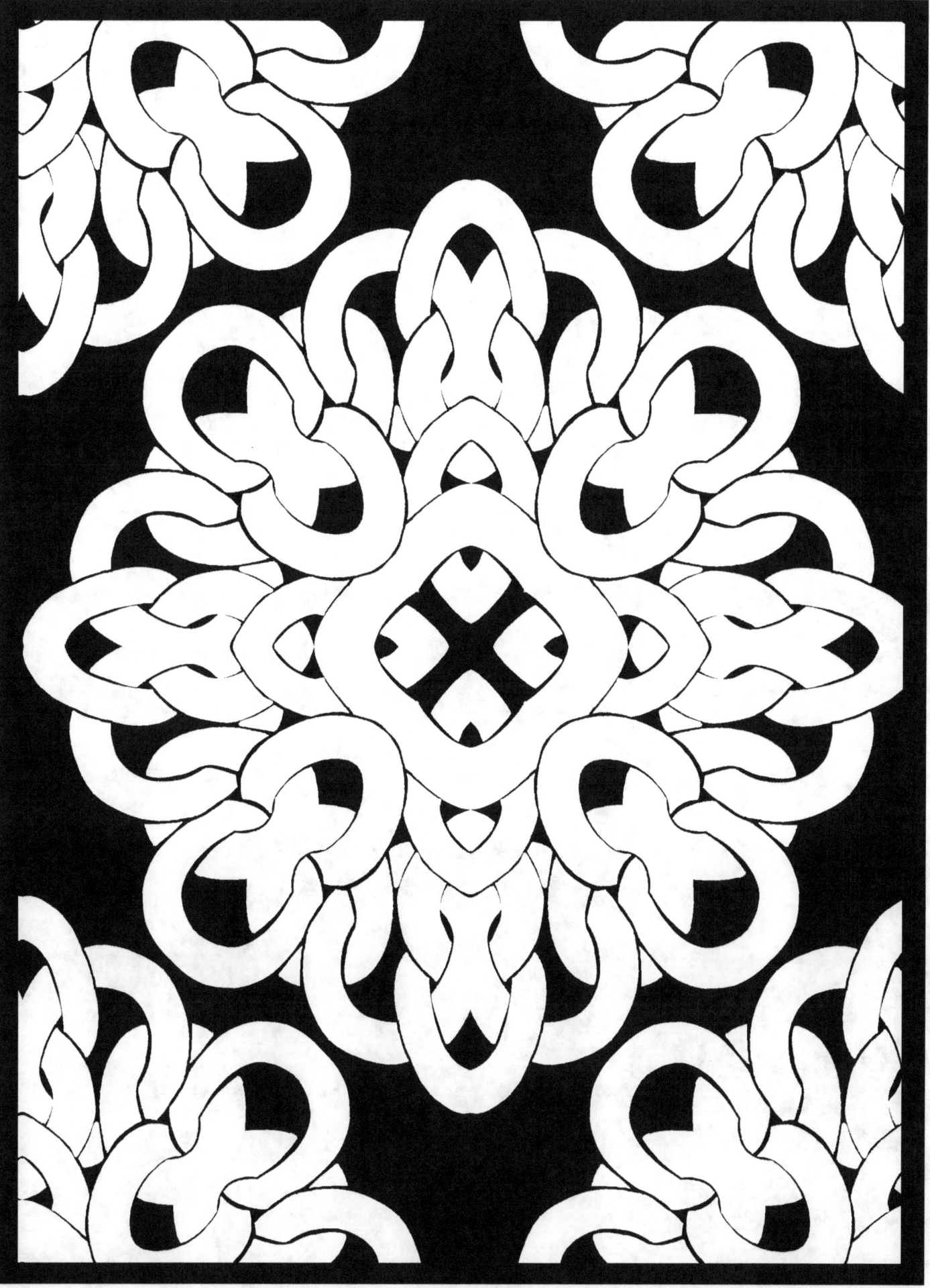

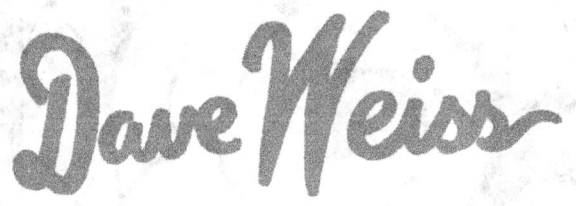

Kaleidoscopics Book 4
"Linked and Braided"

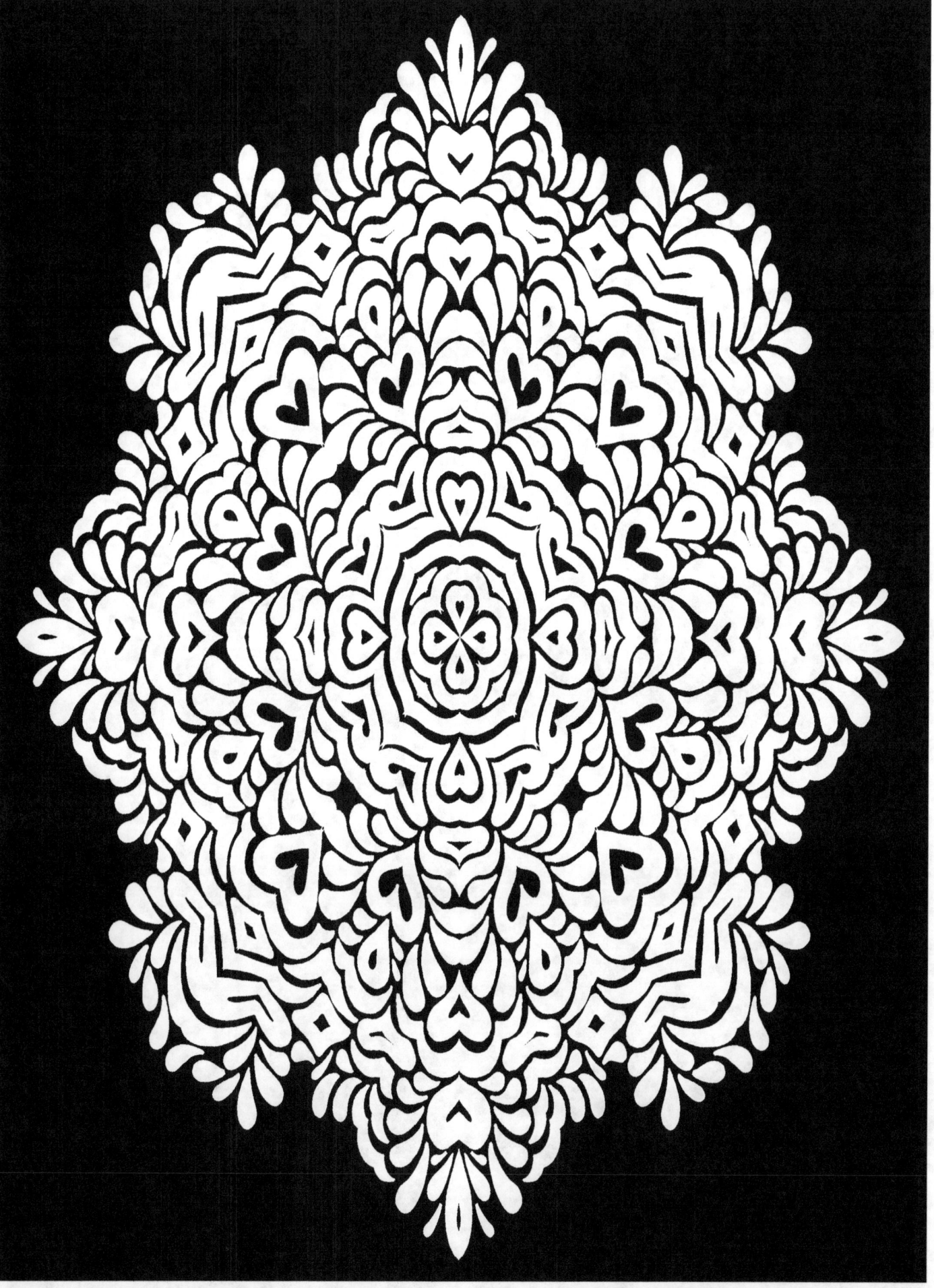

Dave Weiss

Kaleidoscopics Book 4
"Hearts and Flowers"

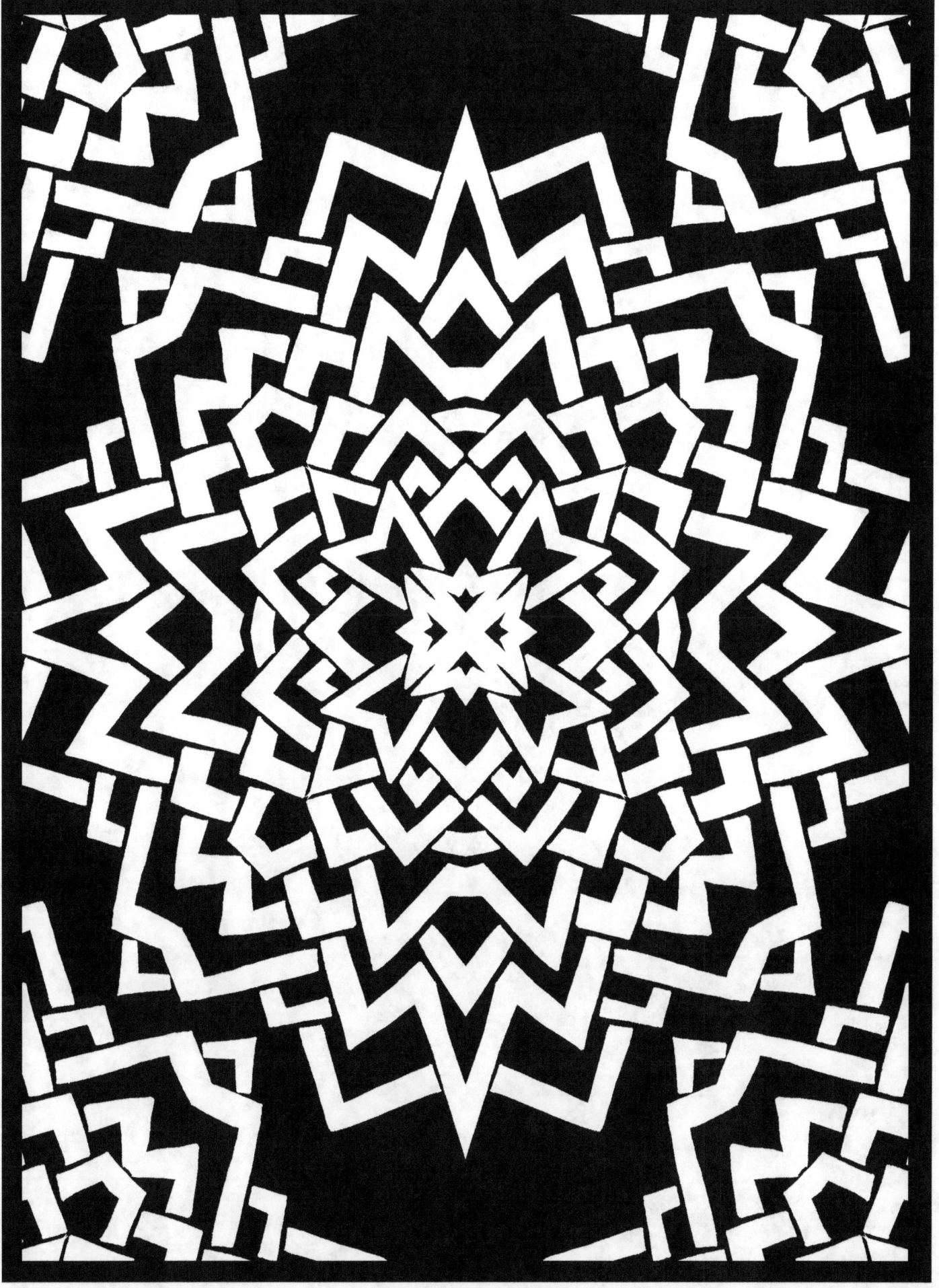

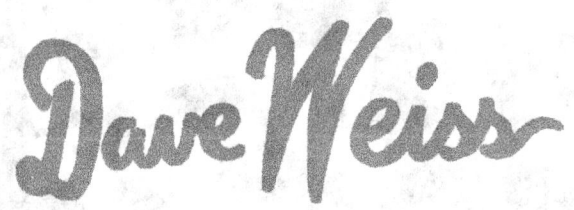

Kaleidoscopics Book 4
"What's Your Point?"

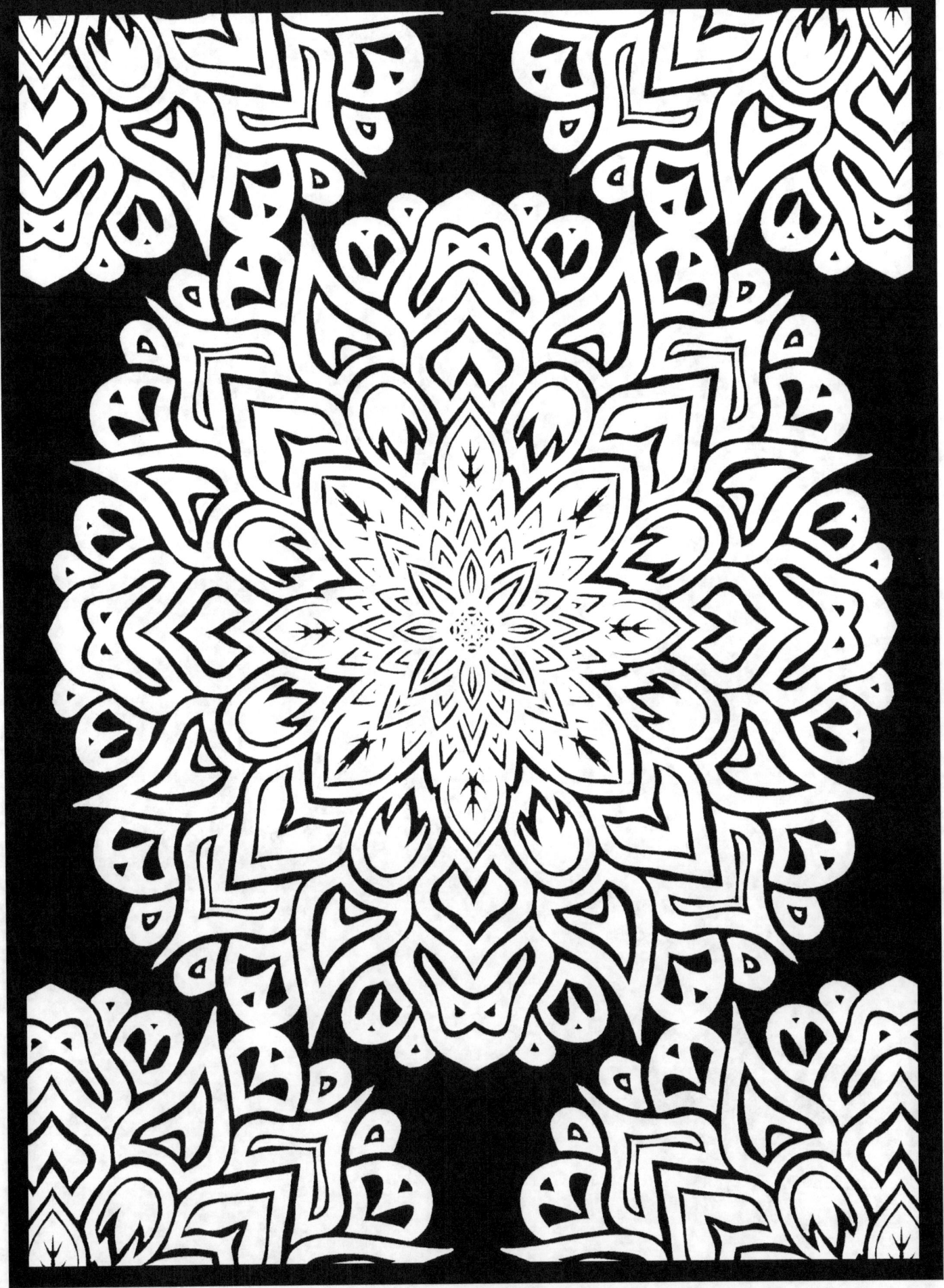

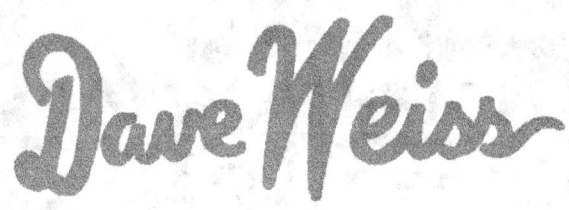

Kaleidoscopics Book 4
"Fracta-Flower"

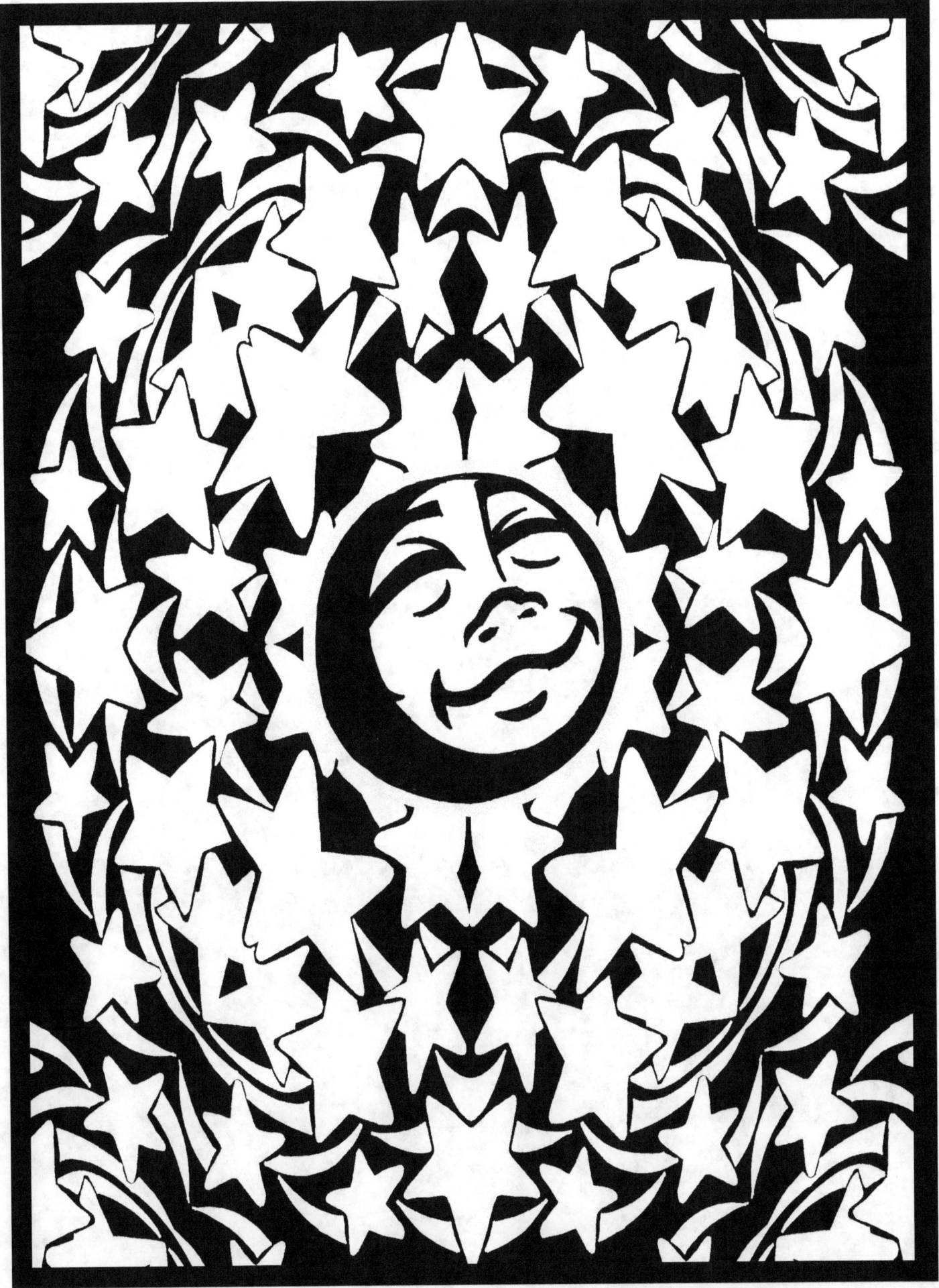

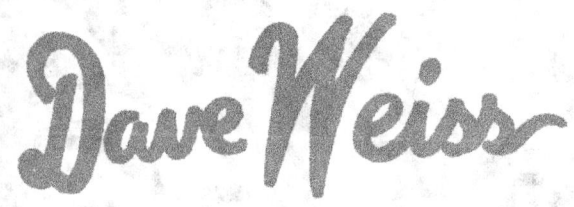

Kaleidoscopics Book 4
"Man On The Moon"

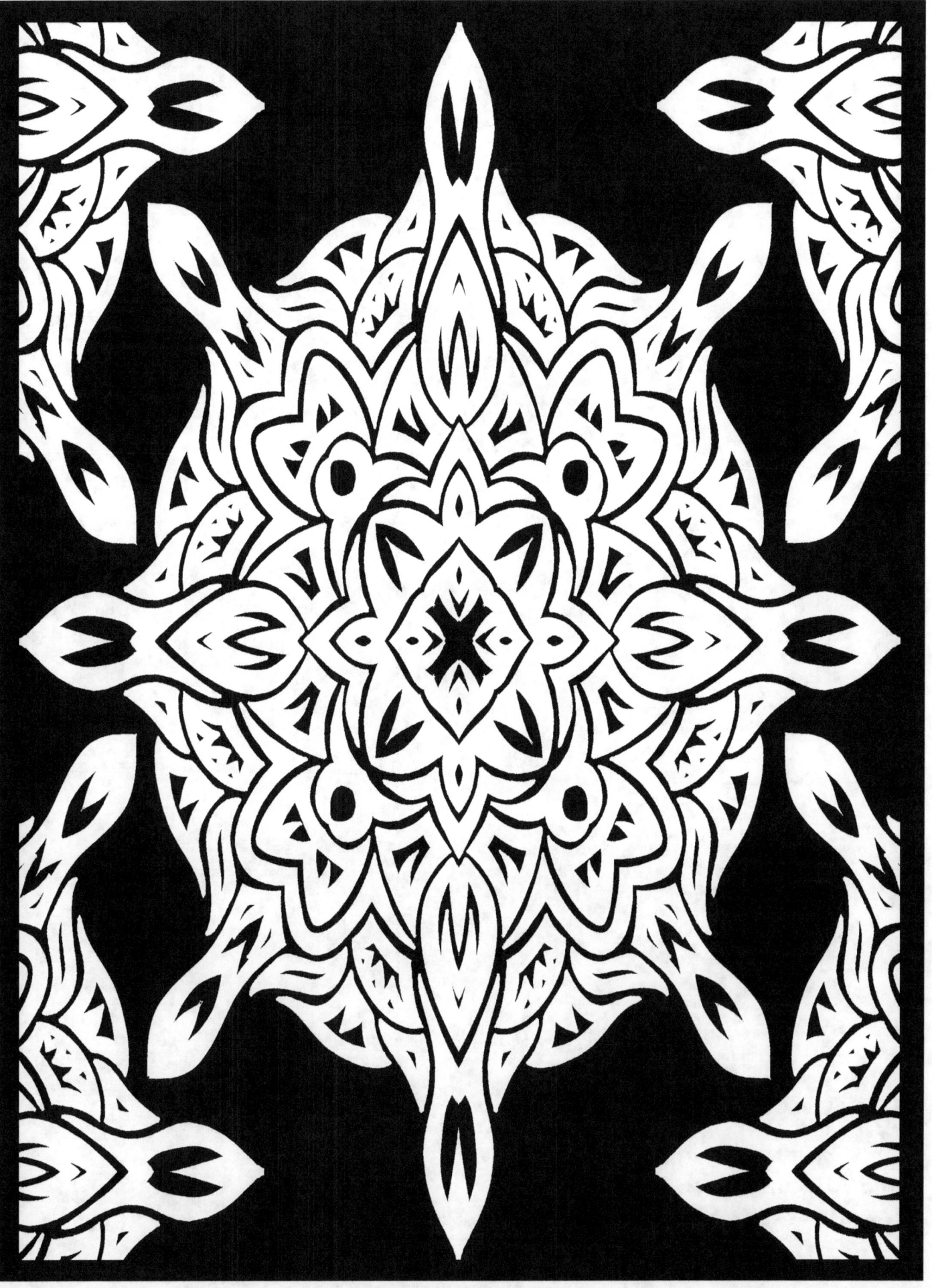

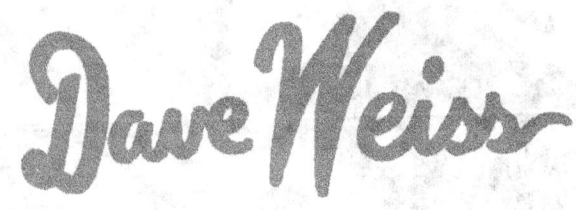

Kaleidoscopics Book 4
"Spooning"

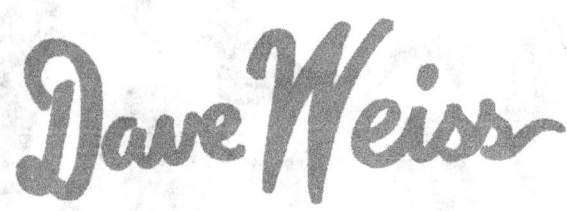

Kaleidoscopics Book 4
"Gracefully Lacy"

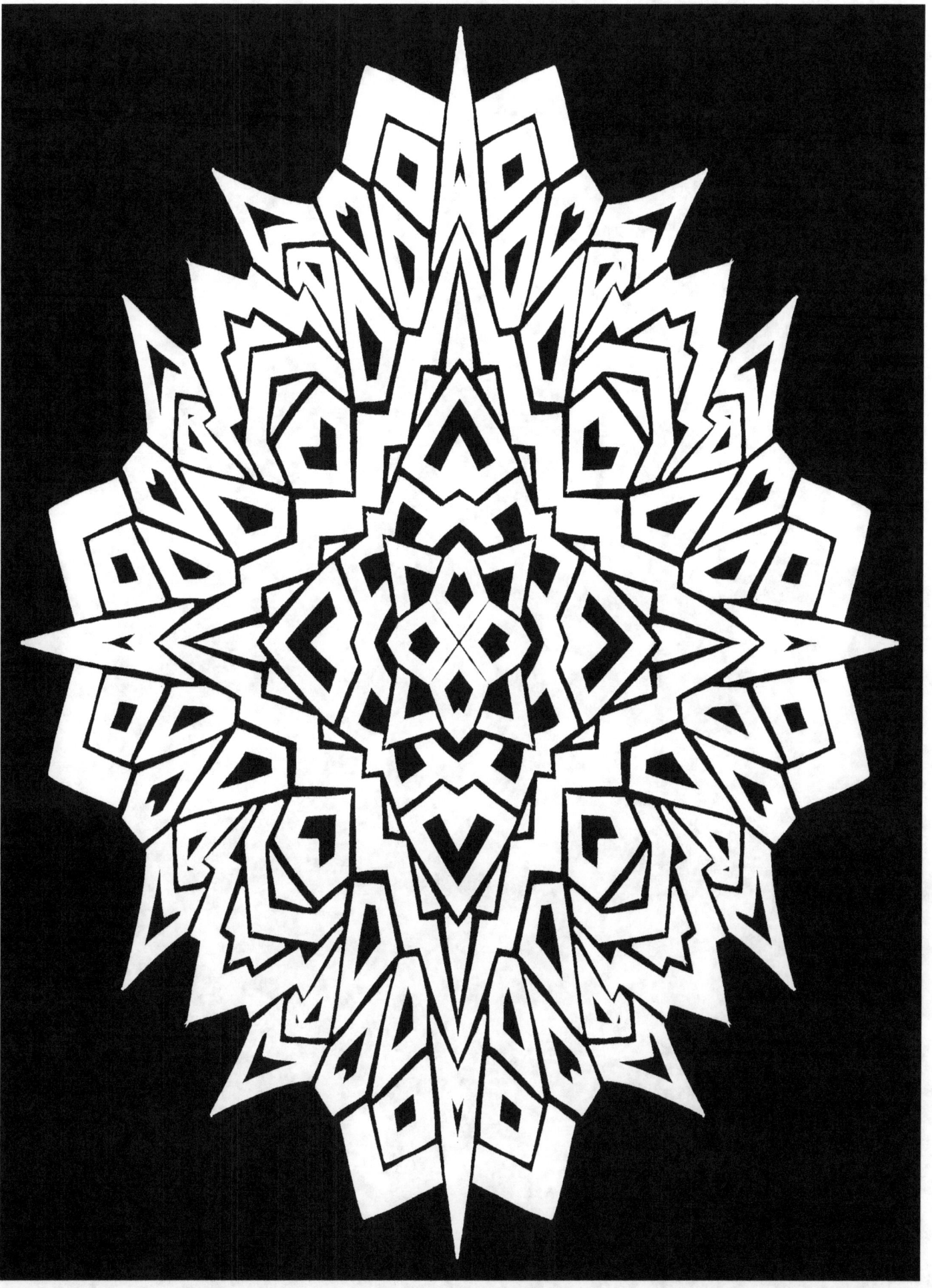

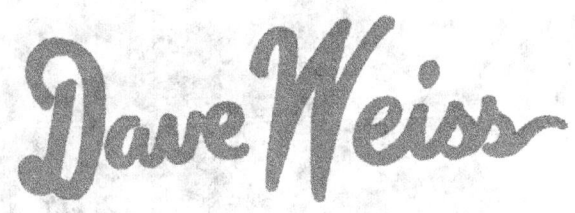

Kaleidoscopics Book 4
"Compass-Ion"

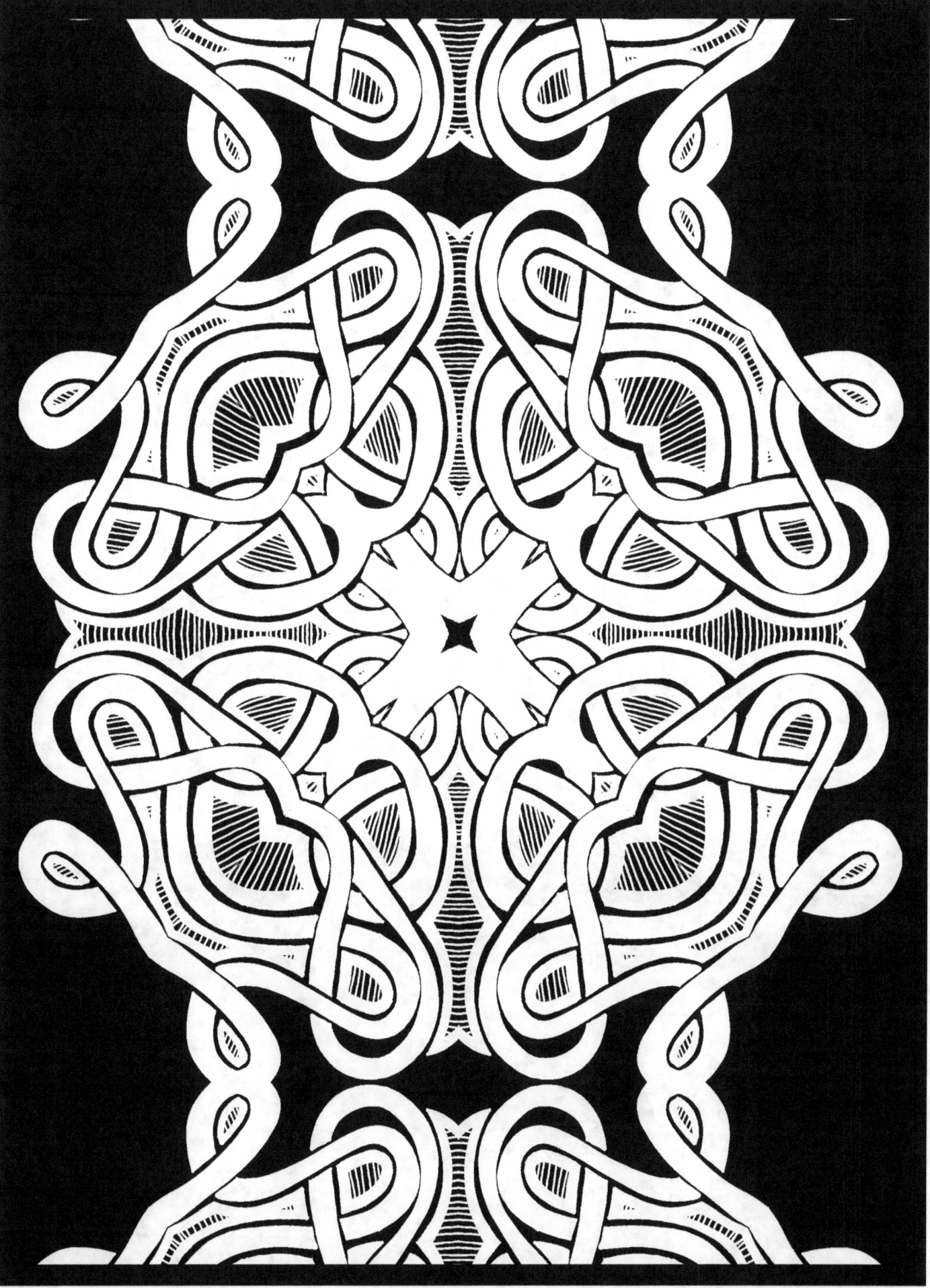

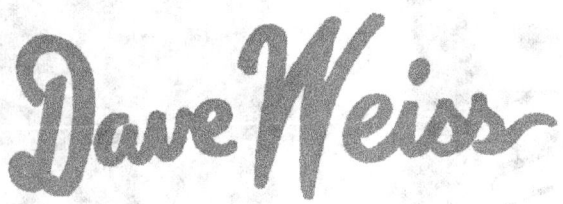

Kaleidoscopics Book 4
"Banded"

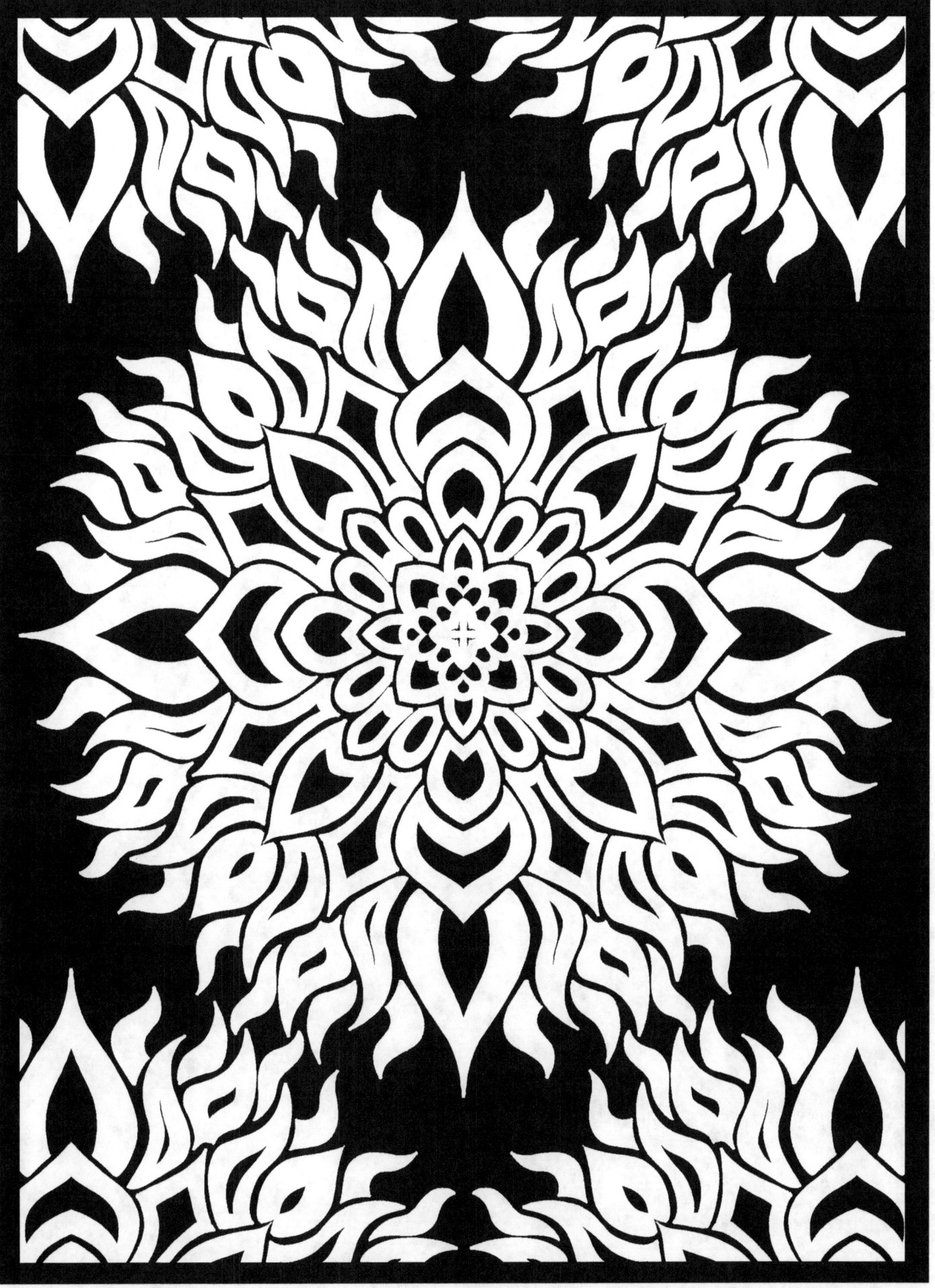

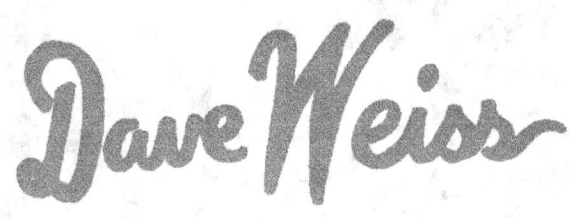

Kaleidoscopics Book 4
"Flamin' Flora"

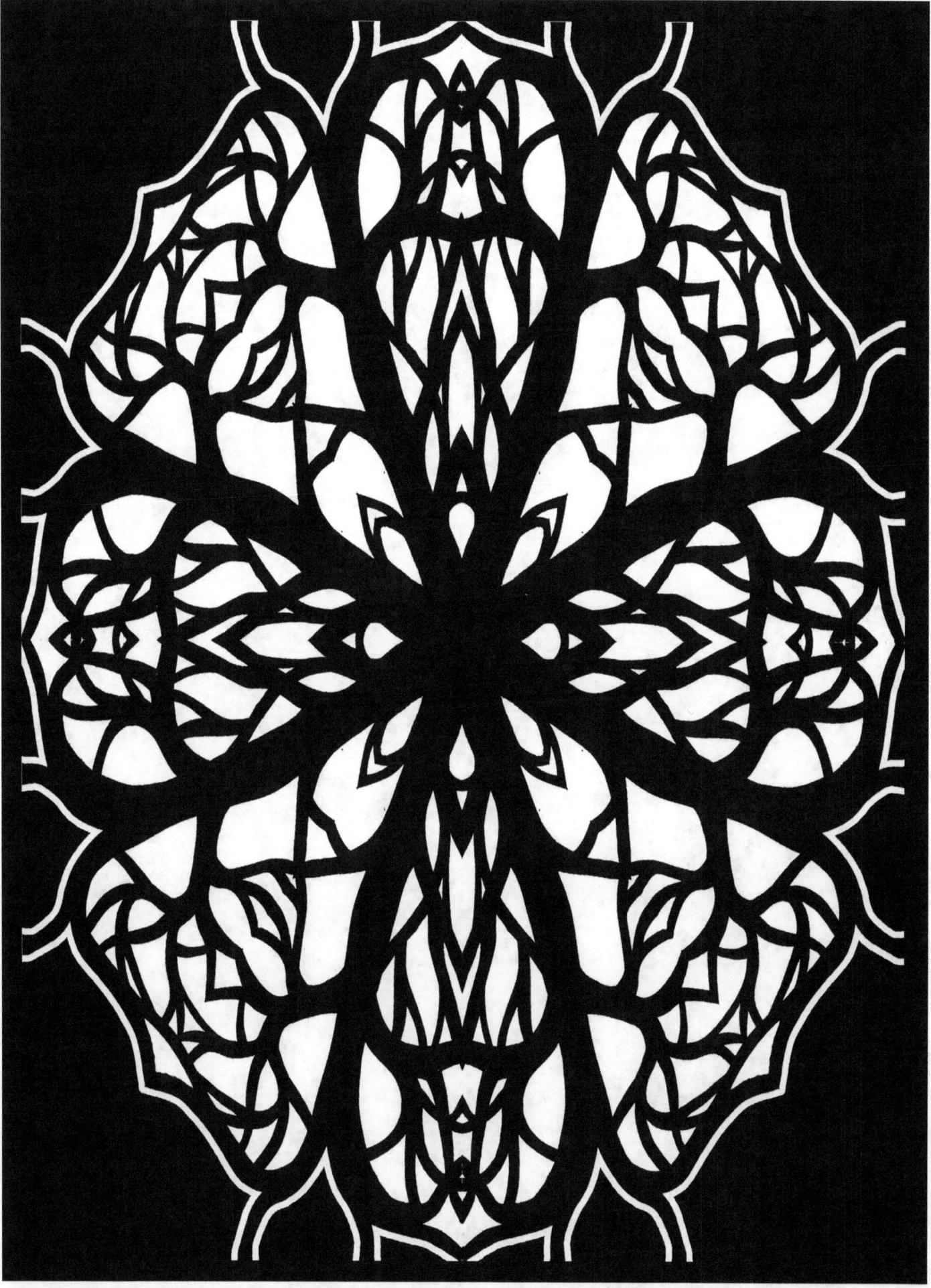

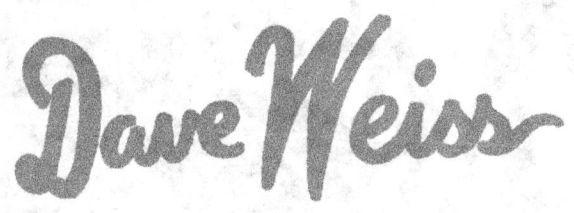

Kaleidoscopics Book 4
"Deep In the Dark, Dark
Wood"

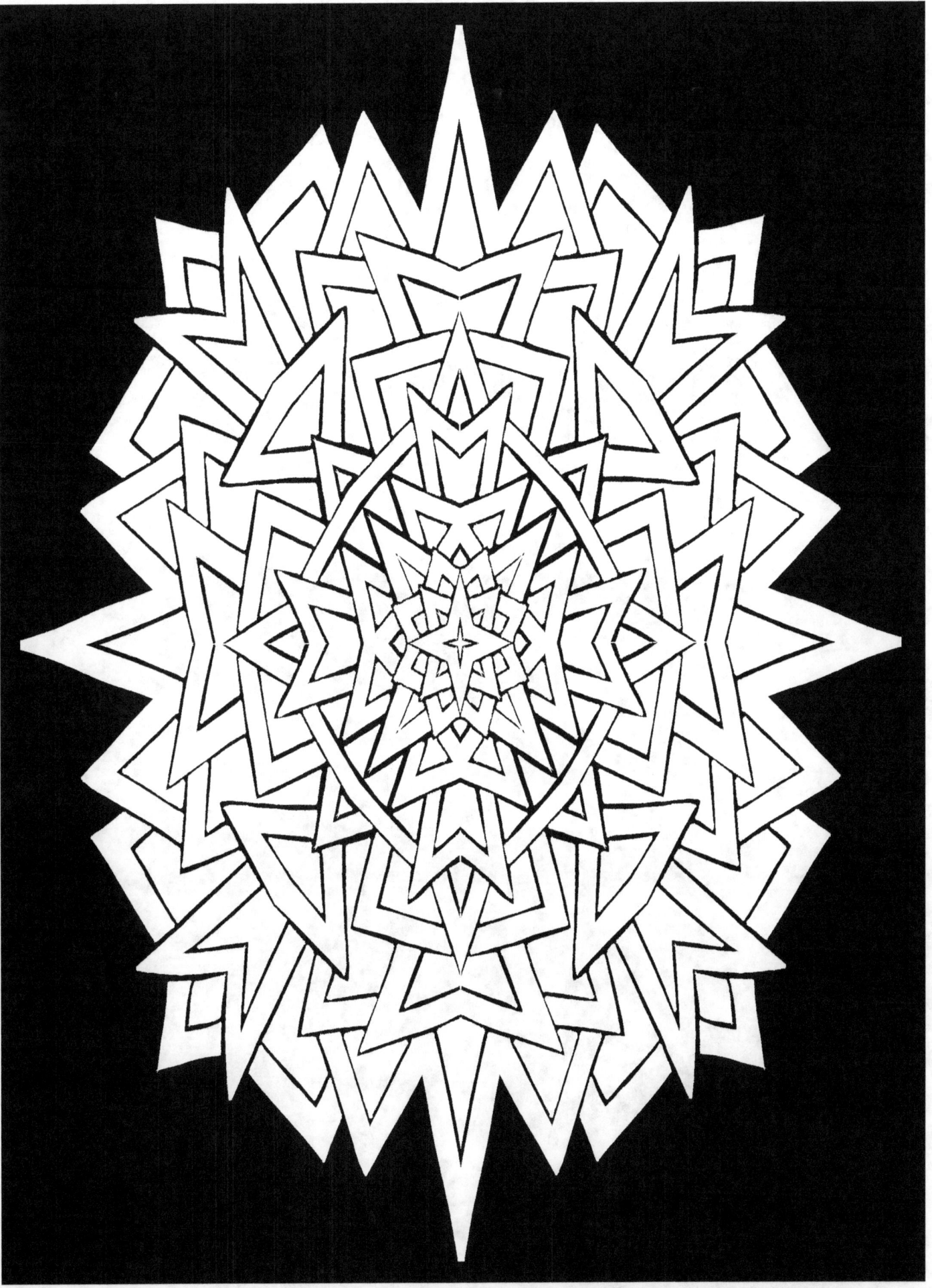

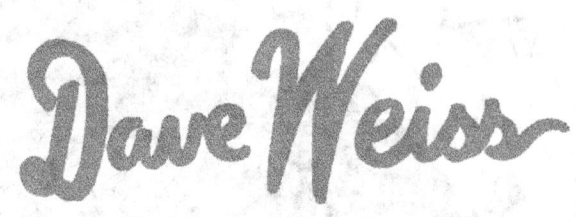

Kaleidoscopics Book 4
"Shield of Faith"

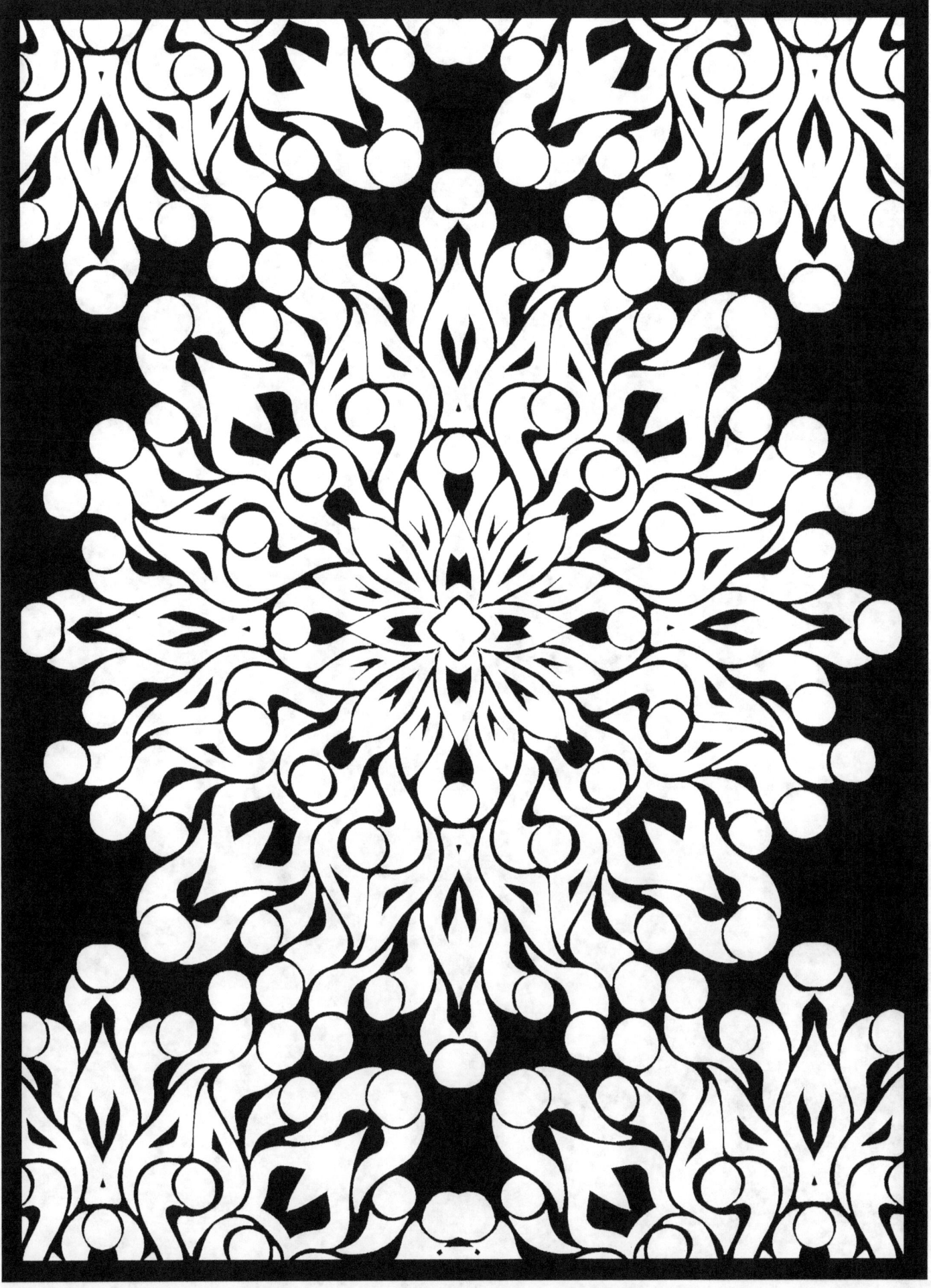

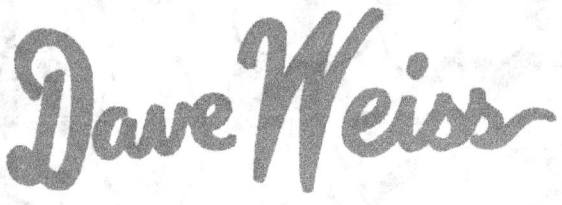

Kaleidoscopics Book 4
"Berries and Blooms"

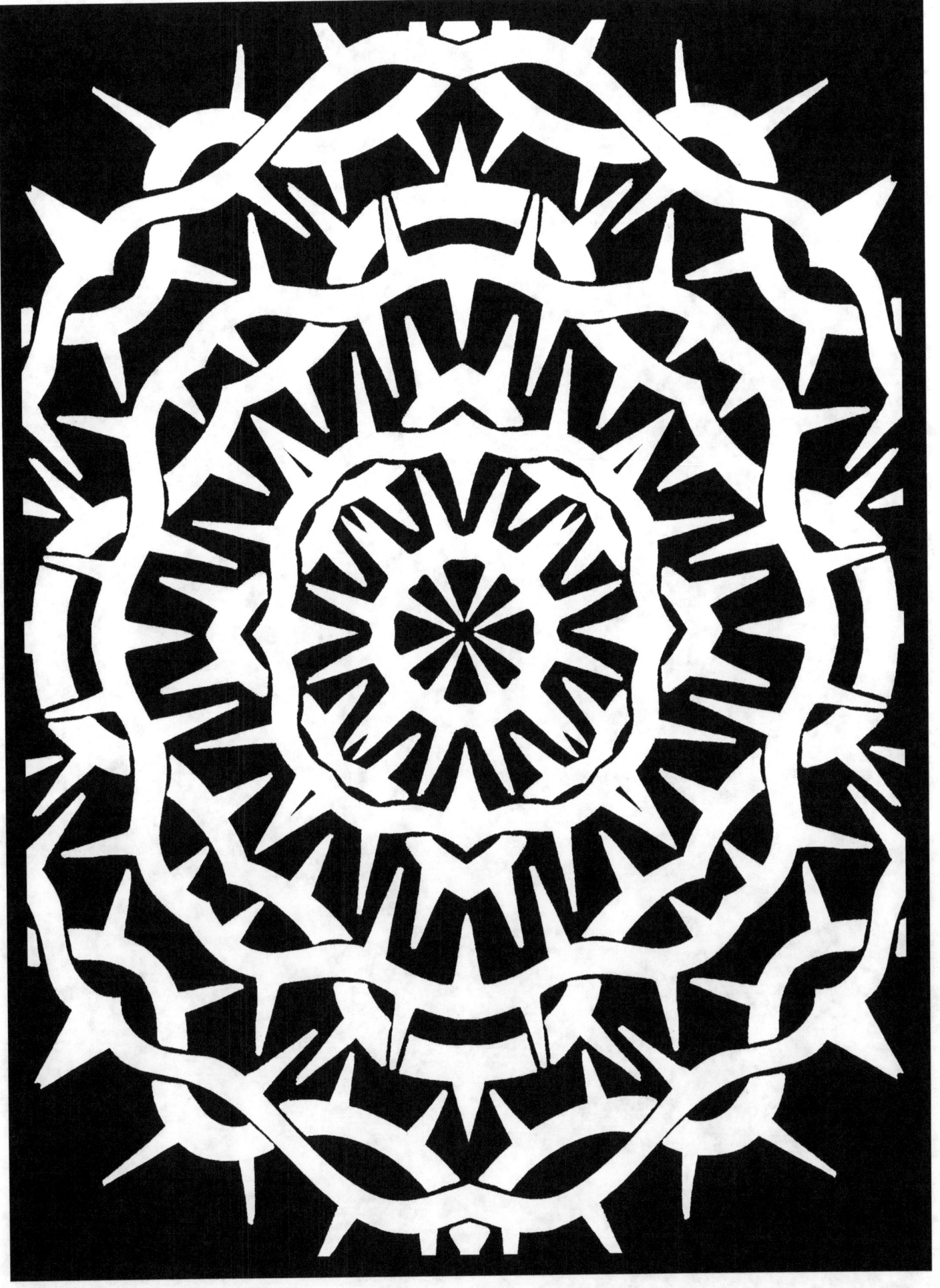

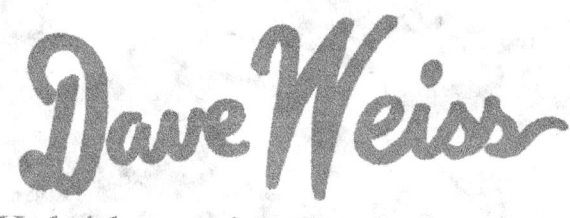

Kaleidoscopics Book 4
"Thorny Issues"

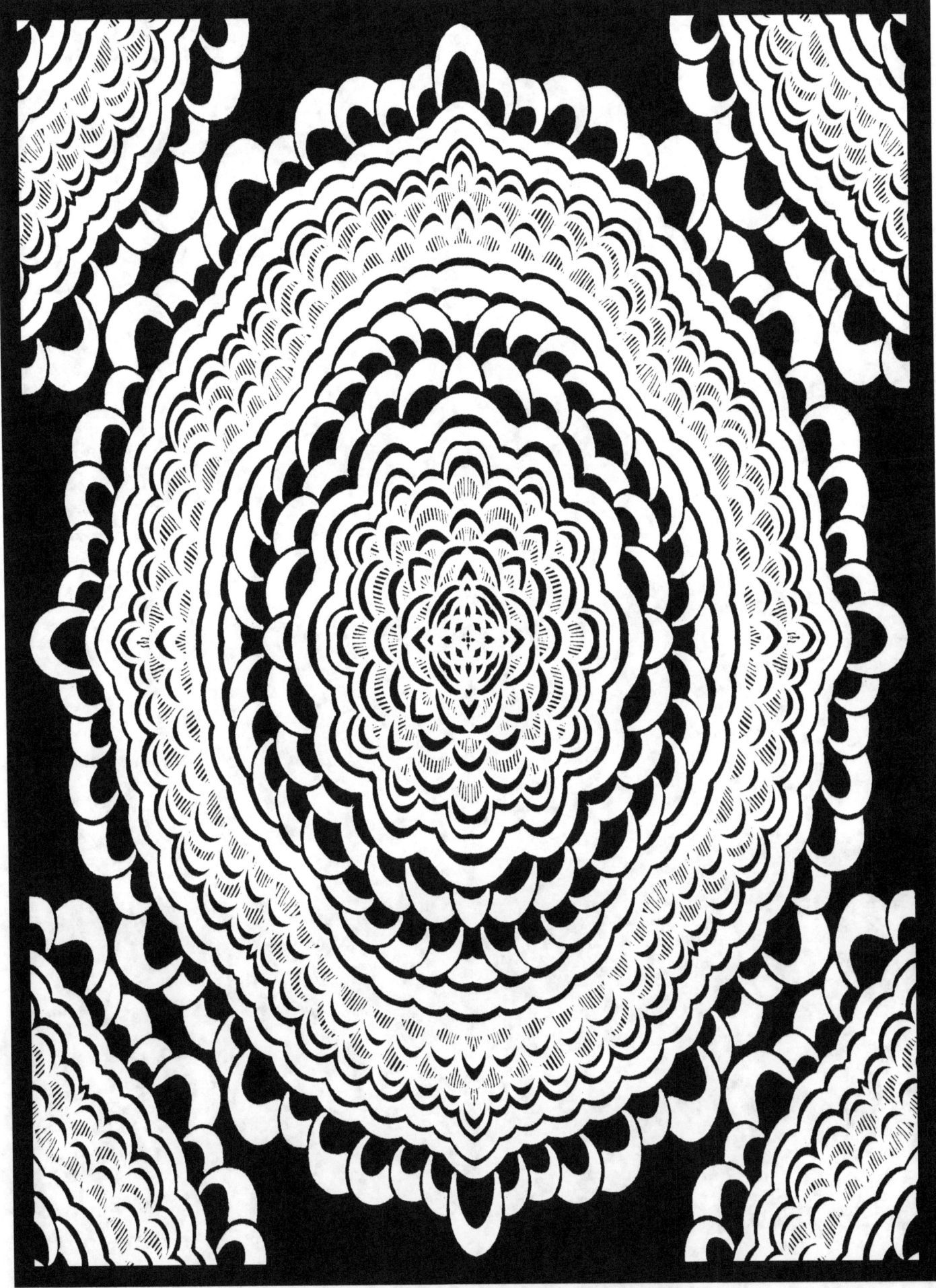

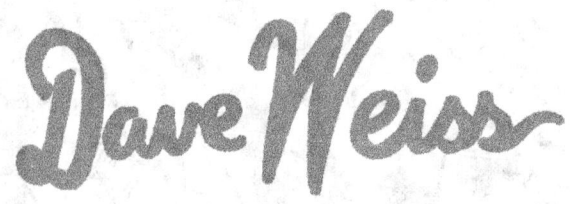

Kaleidoscopics Book 4
"Placemat Placement"

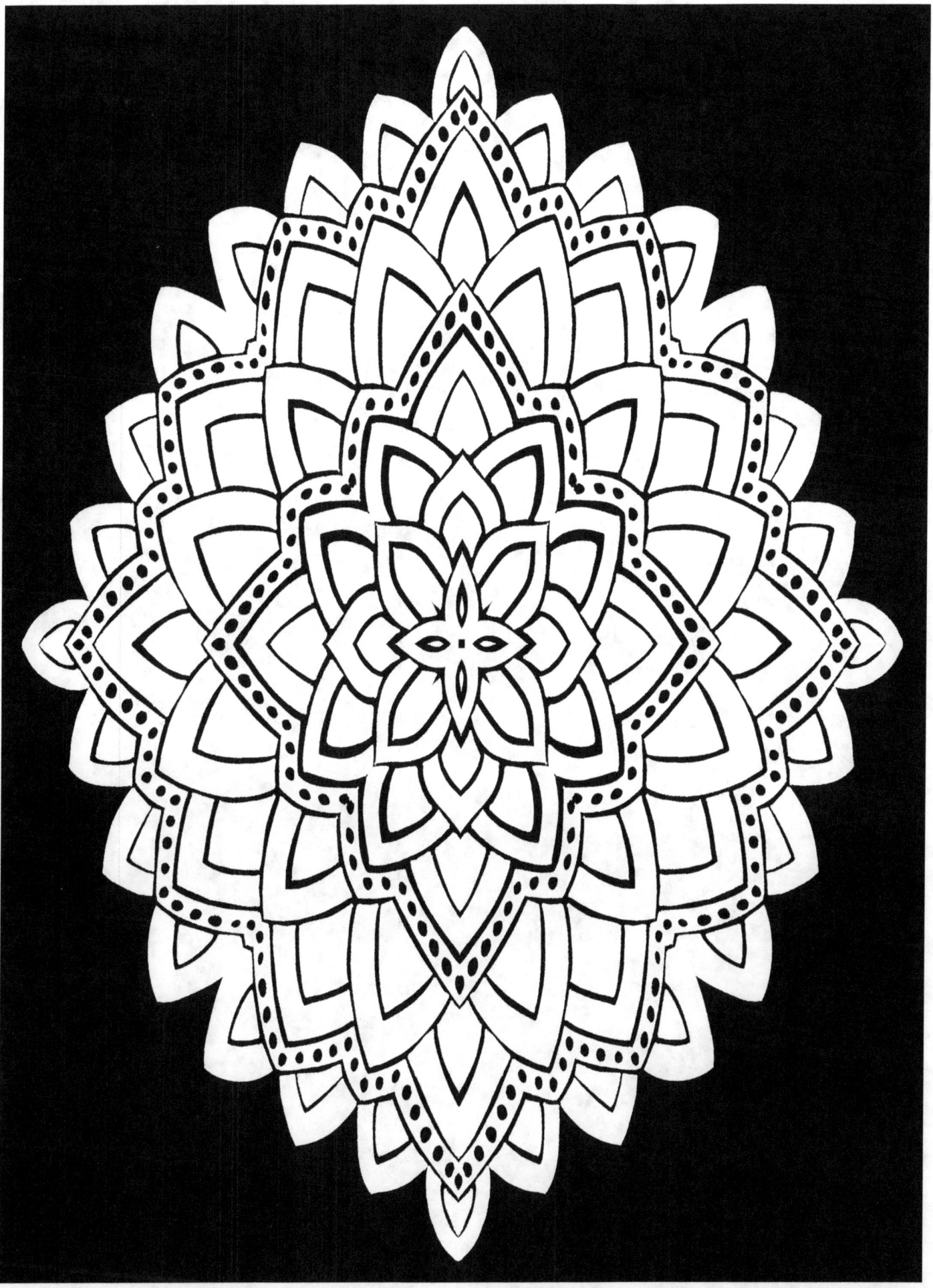

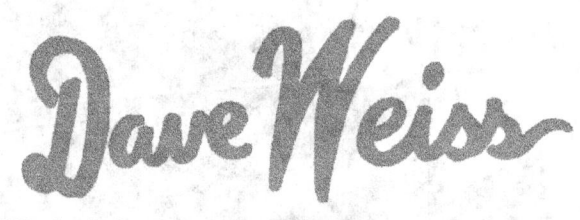

Kaleidoscopics Book 4
"Flourish"

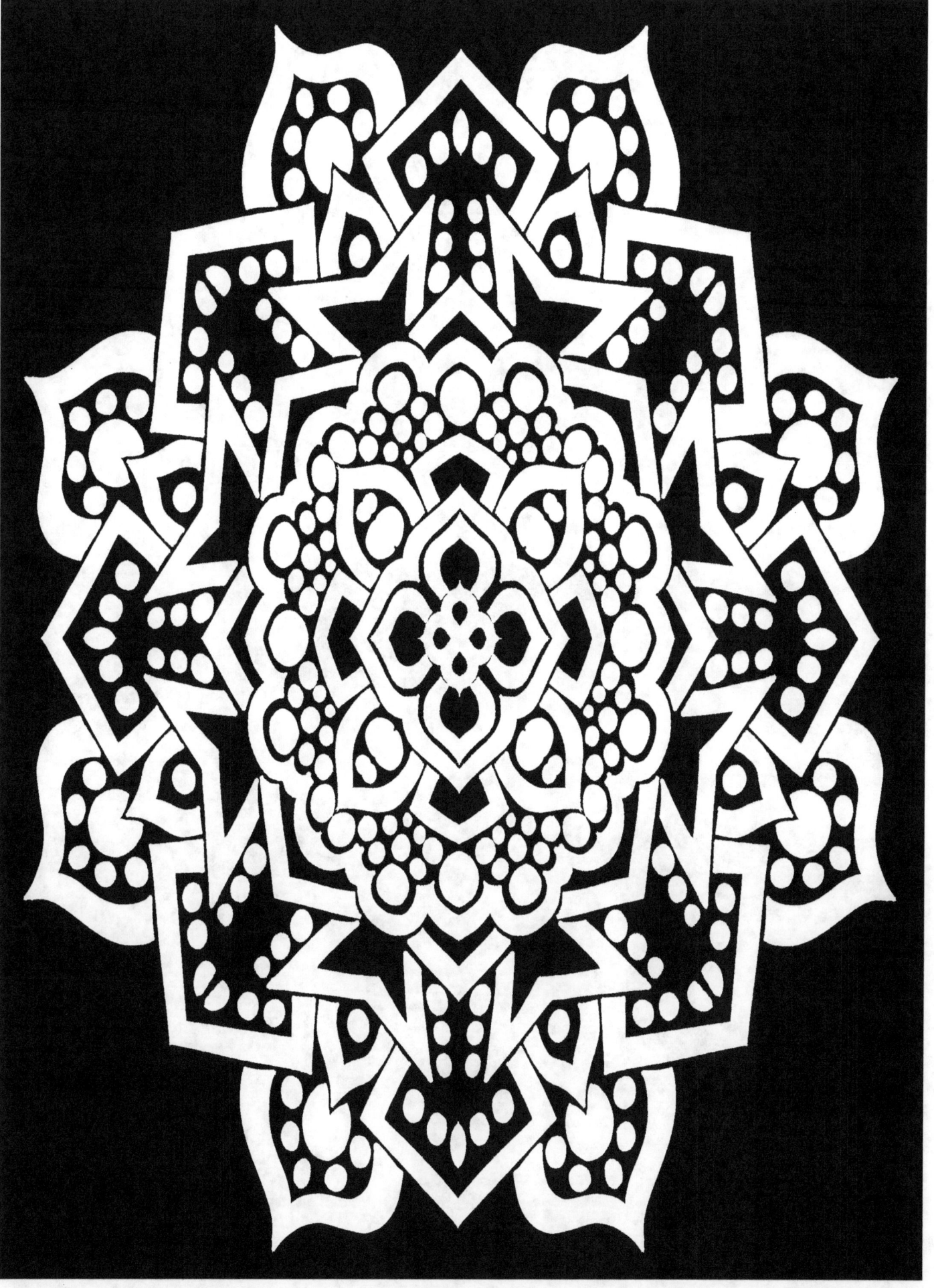

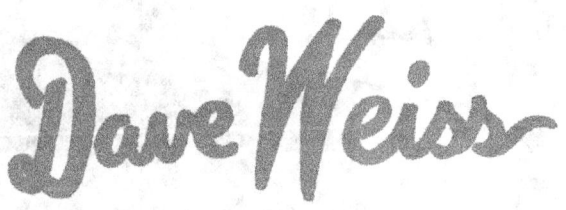

Kaleidoscopics Book 4
"Neon Eon" (Sign of the
Times)

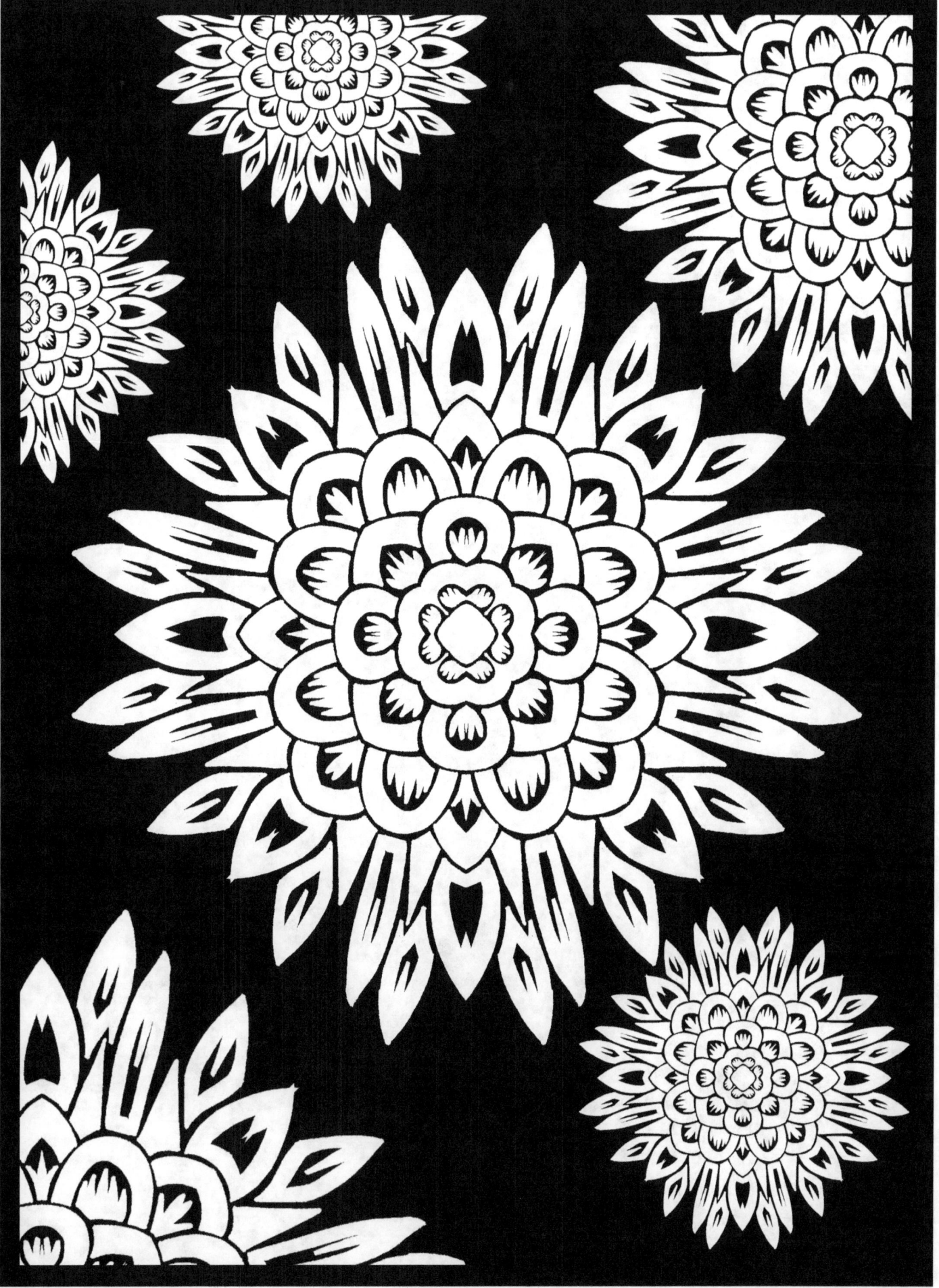

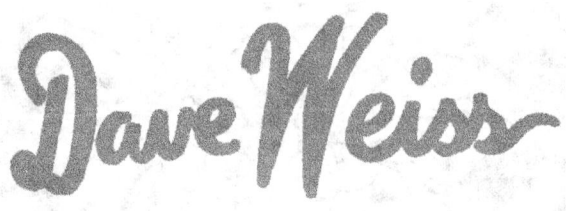

Kaleidoscopics Book 4
"Hydrangeaism"

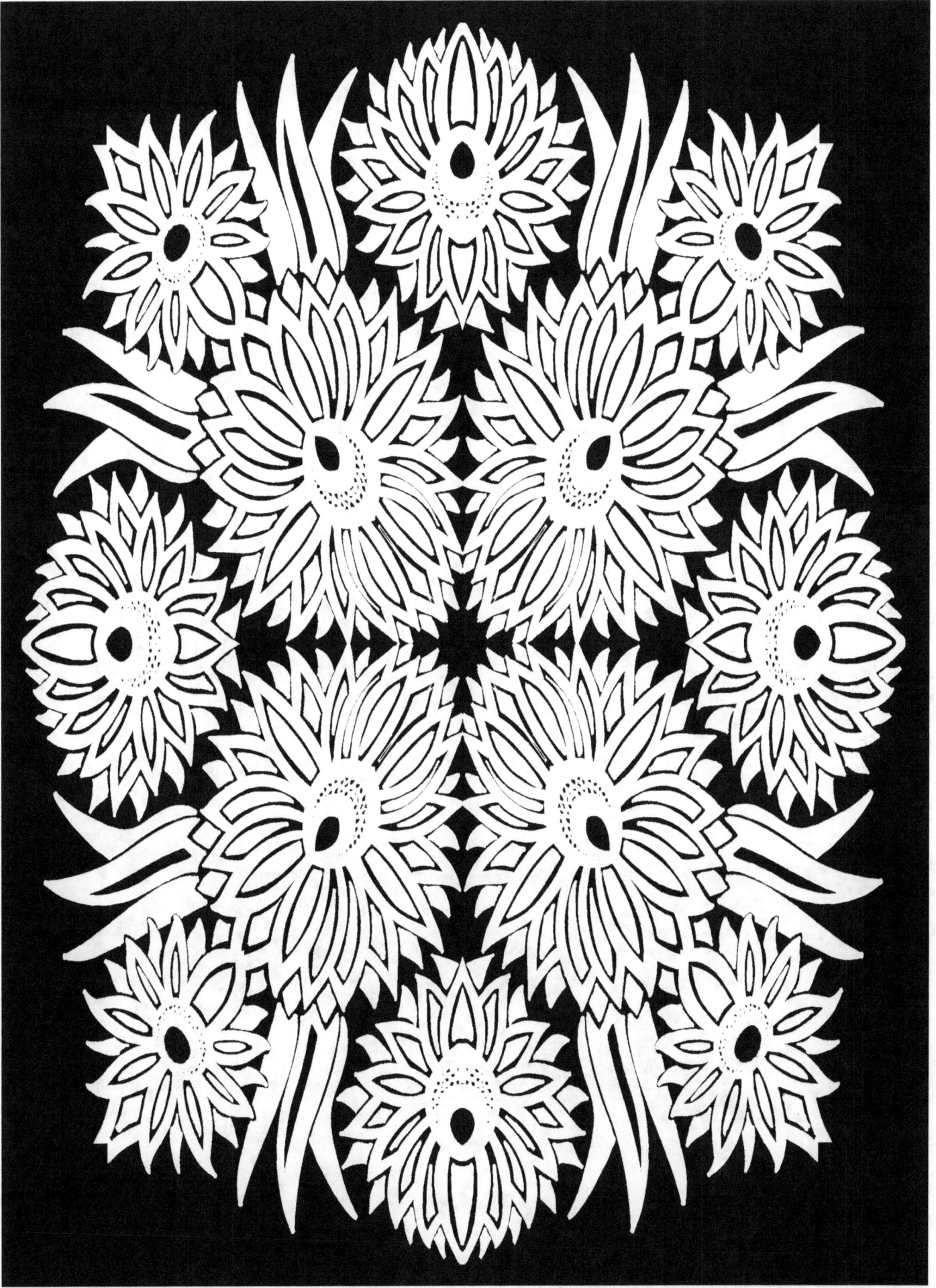

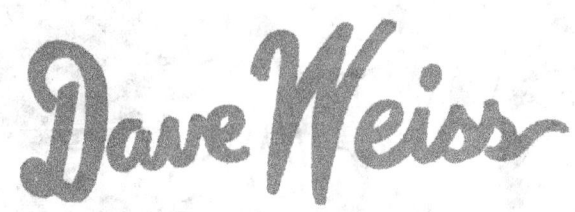

Kaleidoscopics Book 4
"Daised"

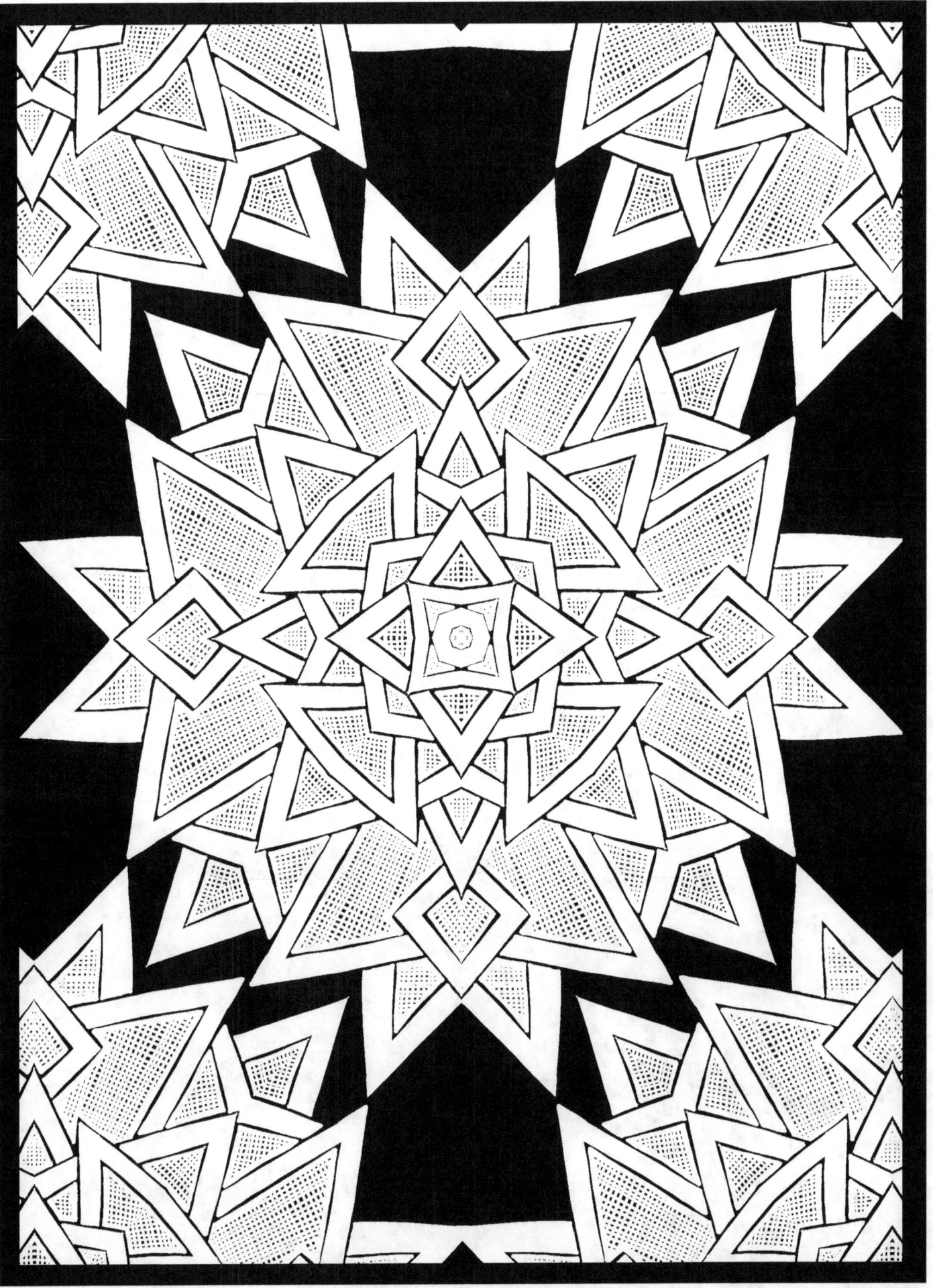

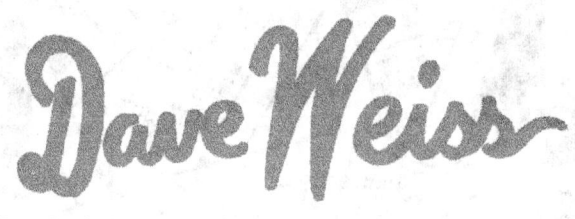

Kaleidoscopics Book 4
"Angle Tangle"

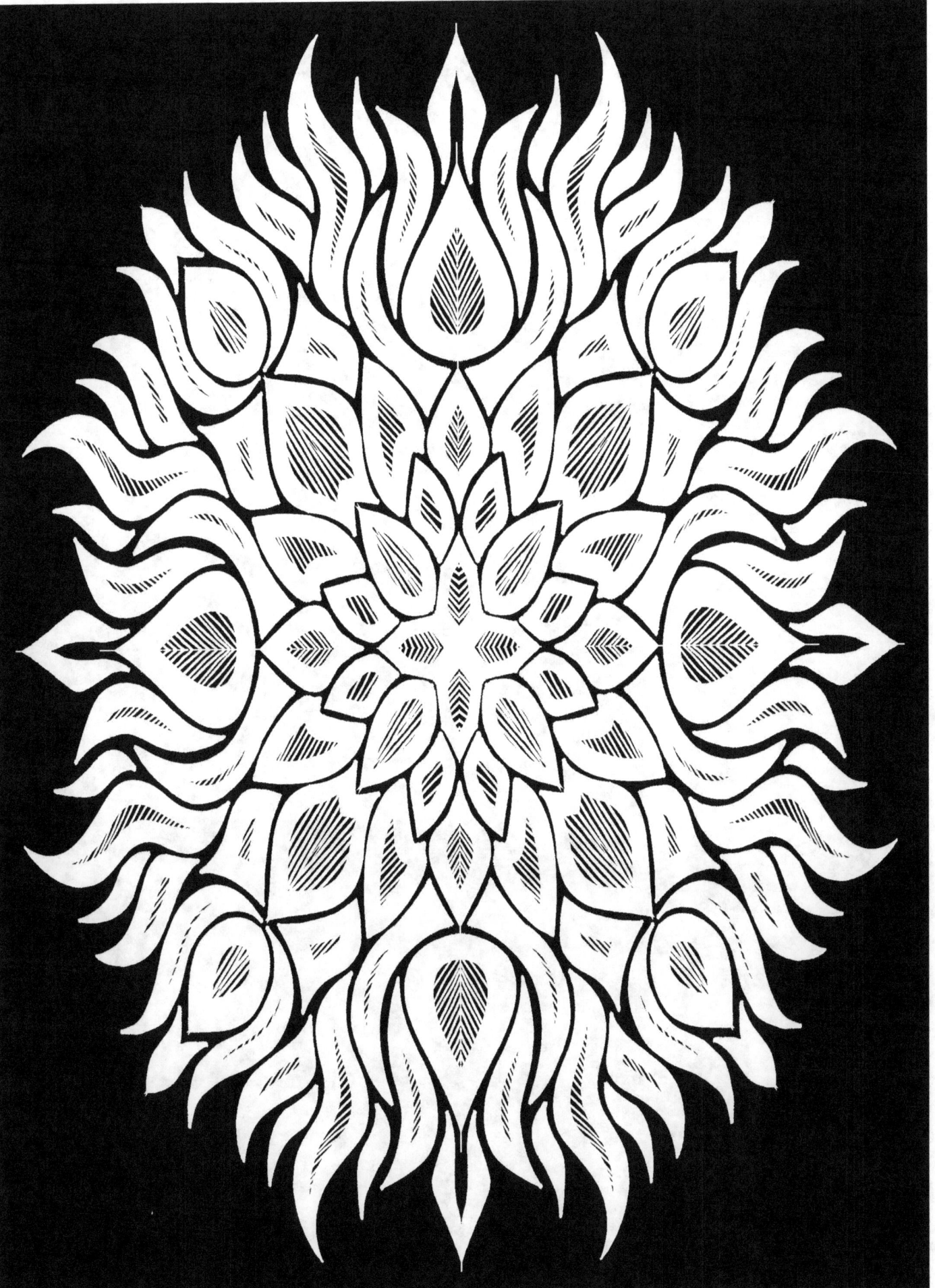

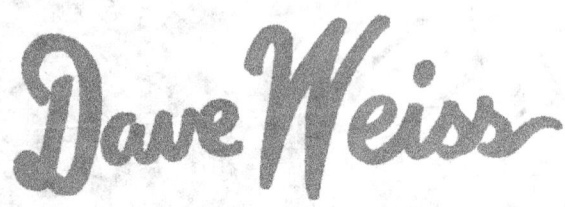

Kaleidoscopics Book 4
"Chrysanthebomb"

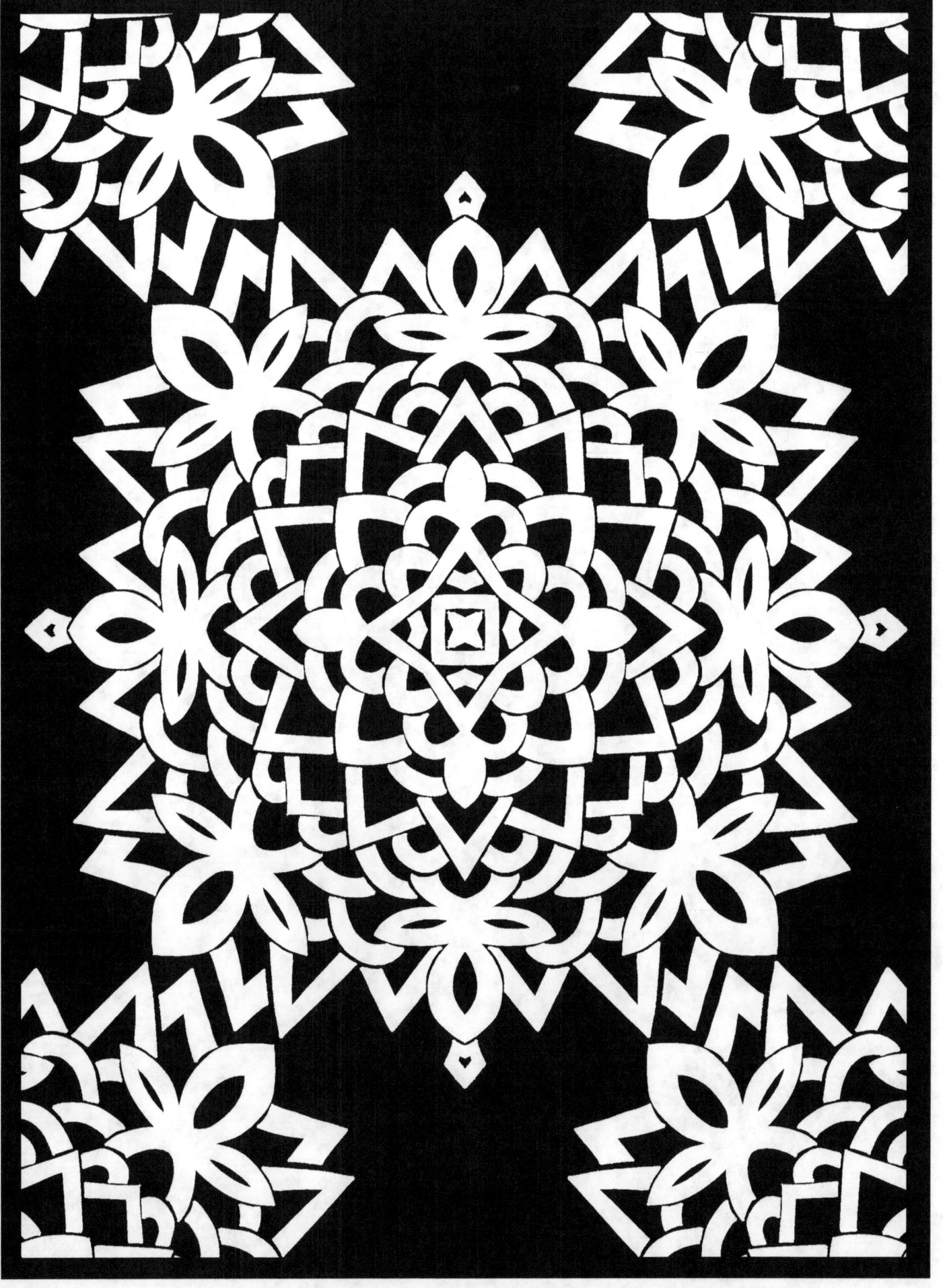

Dave Weiss

Kaleidoscopics Book 4
"Ornately Ornate"

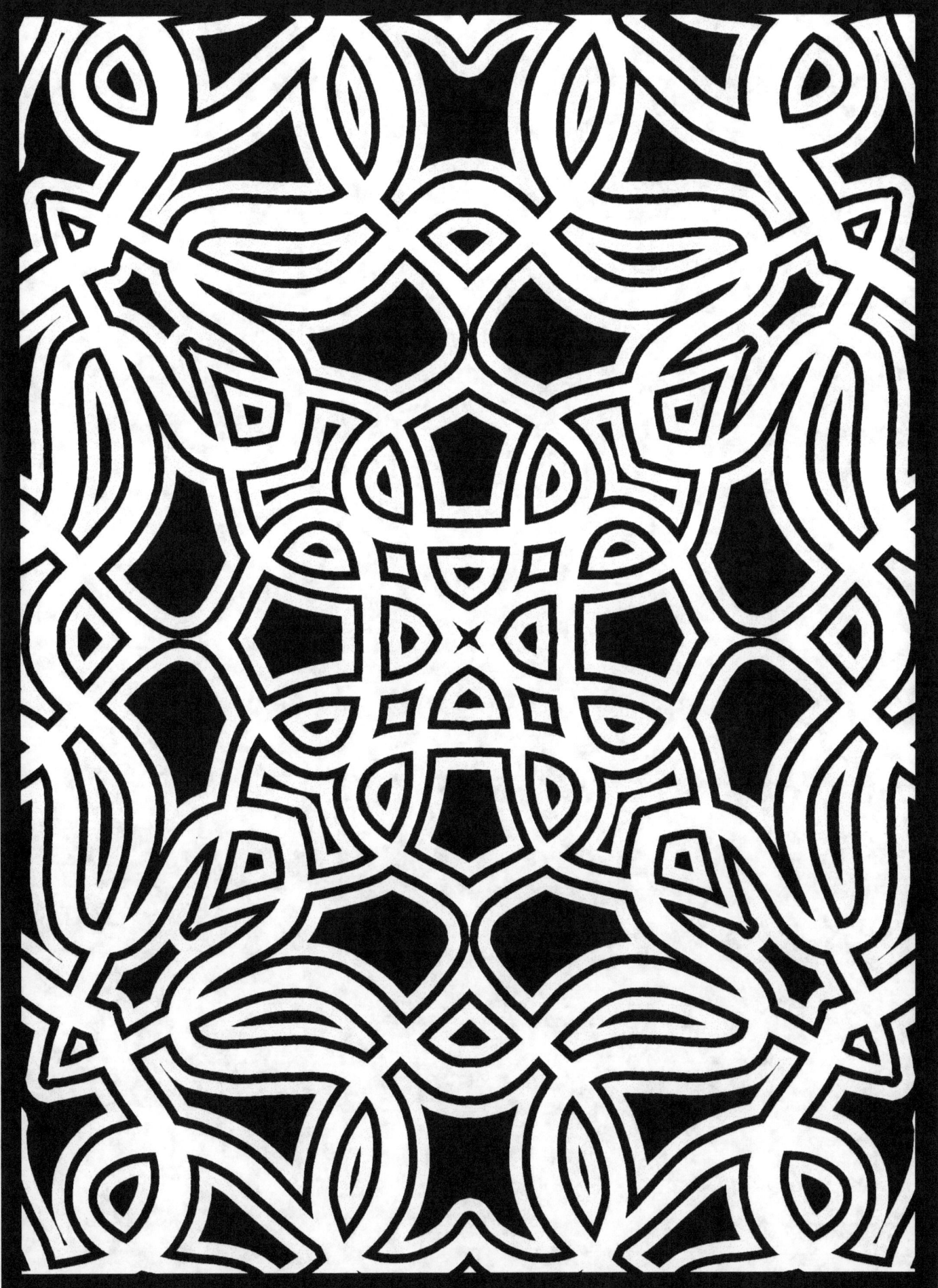

Dave Weiss

Kaleidoscopics Book 4
"Tangible Tangle"

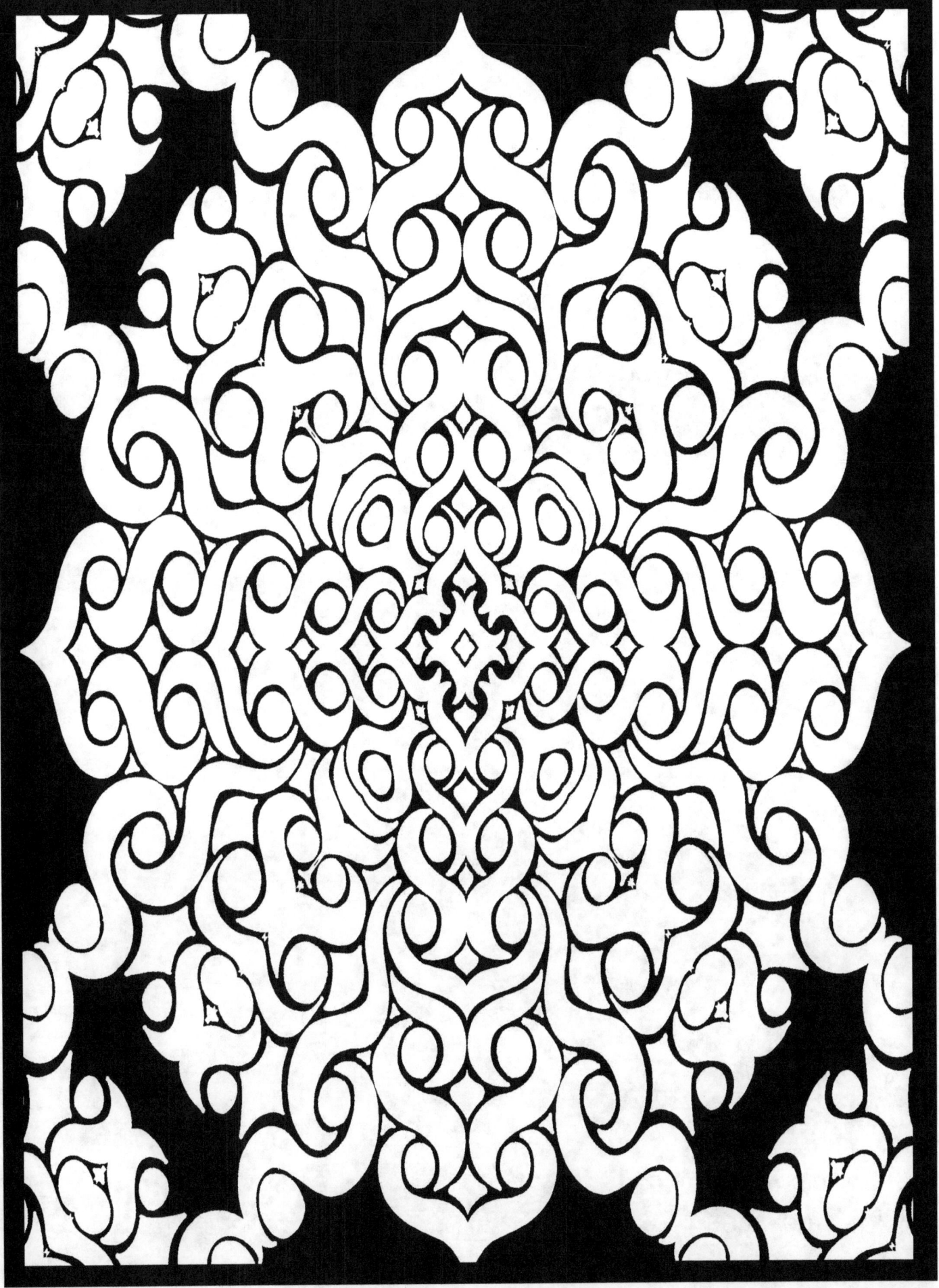

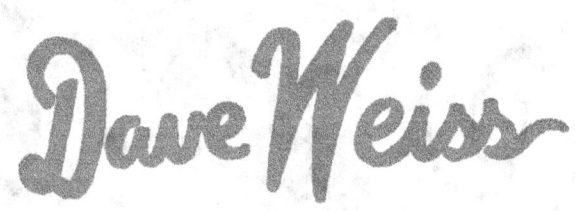

Kaleidoscopics Book 4
"Swirls and Pearls"

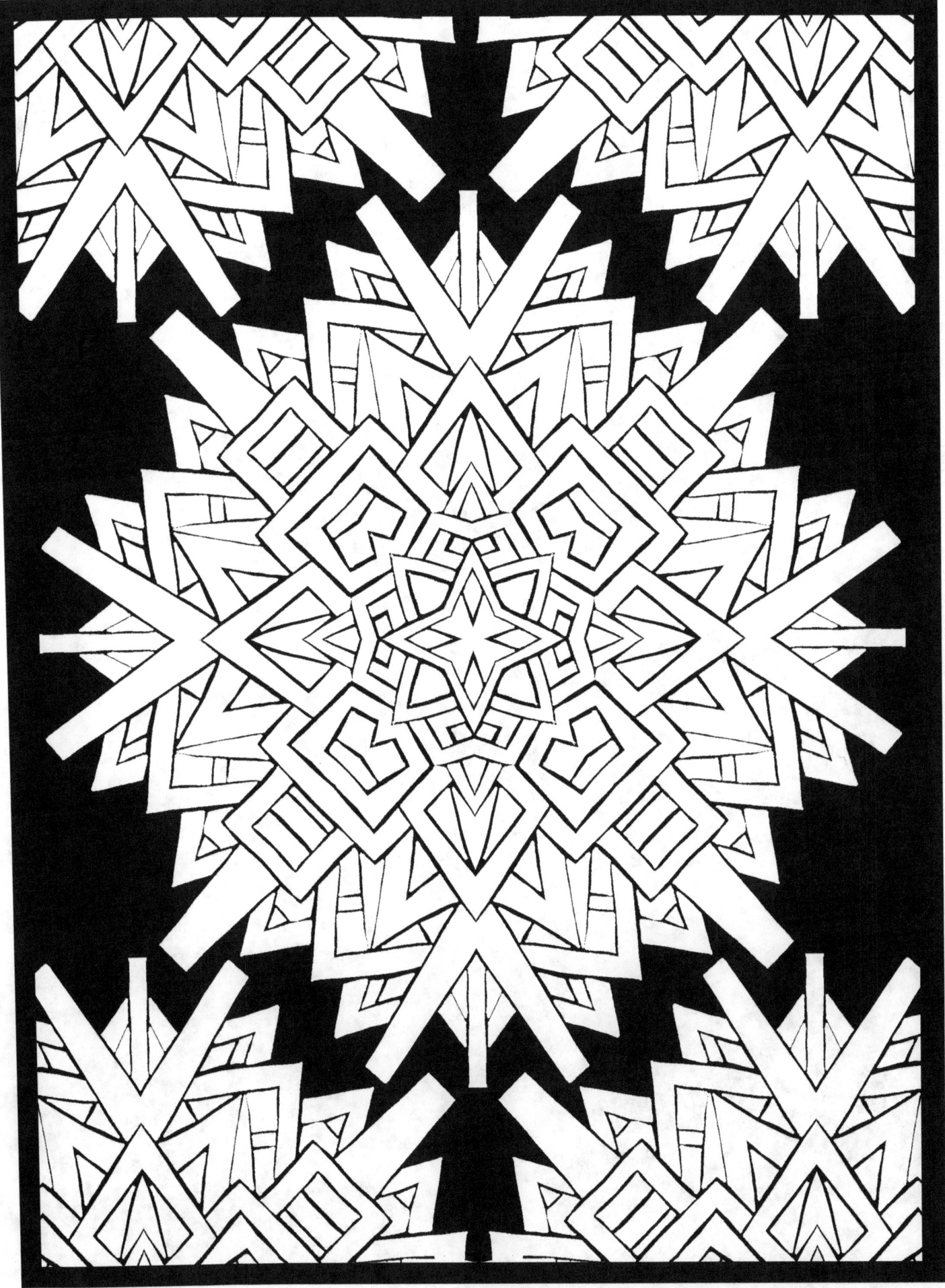

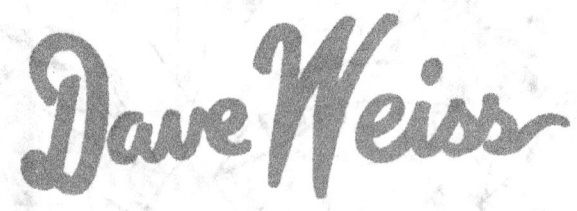

Kaleidoscopics Book 4
"Feelin' Flaky"

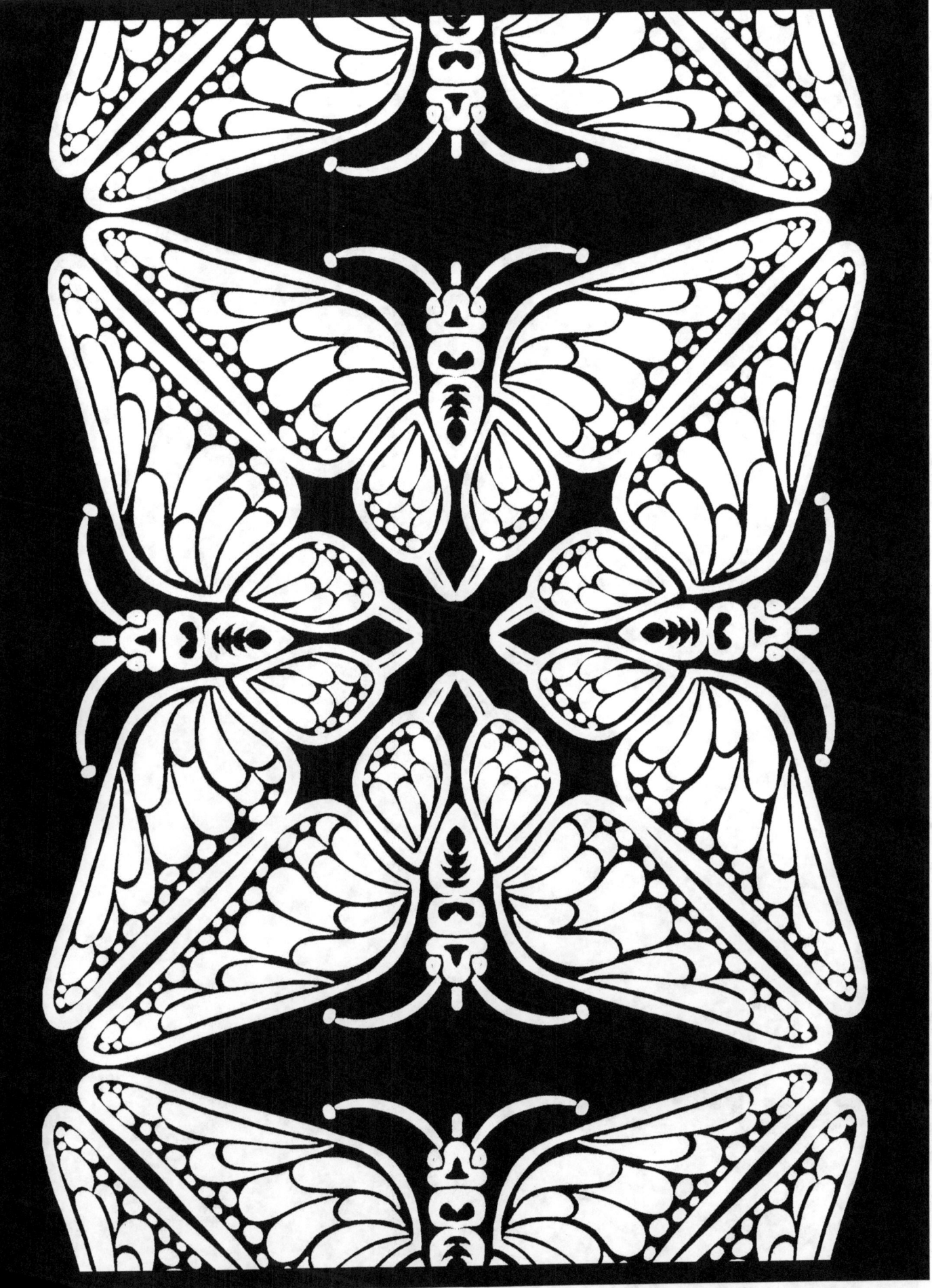

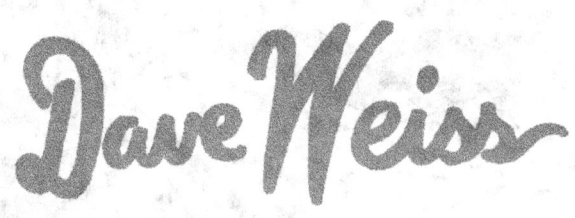

Kaleidoscopics Book 4
"Flutterby"

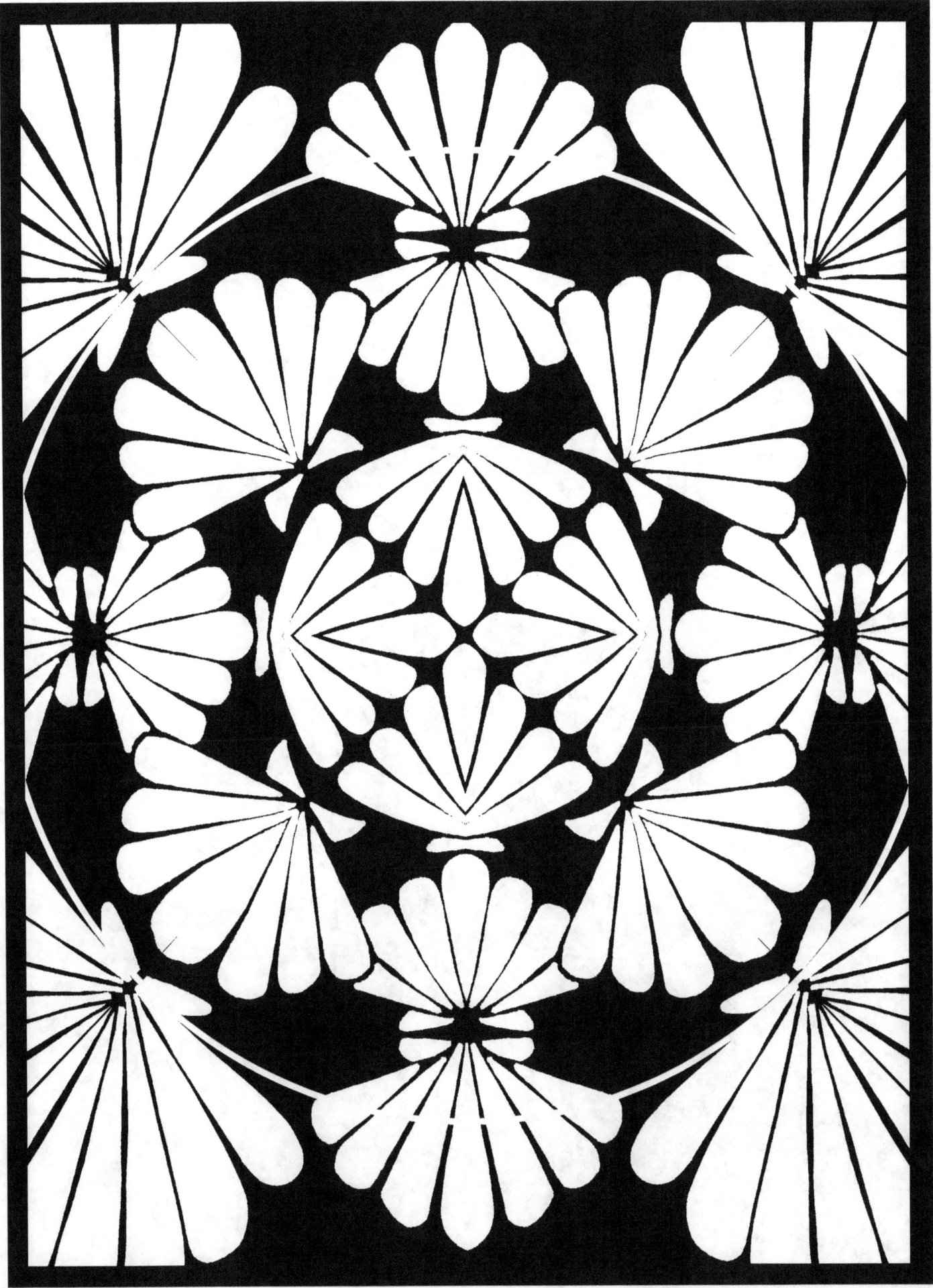

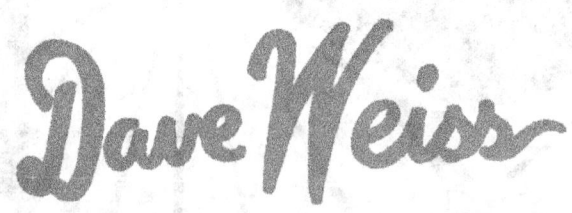

Kaleidoscopics Book 4
"Scalloped"

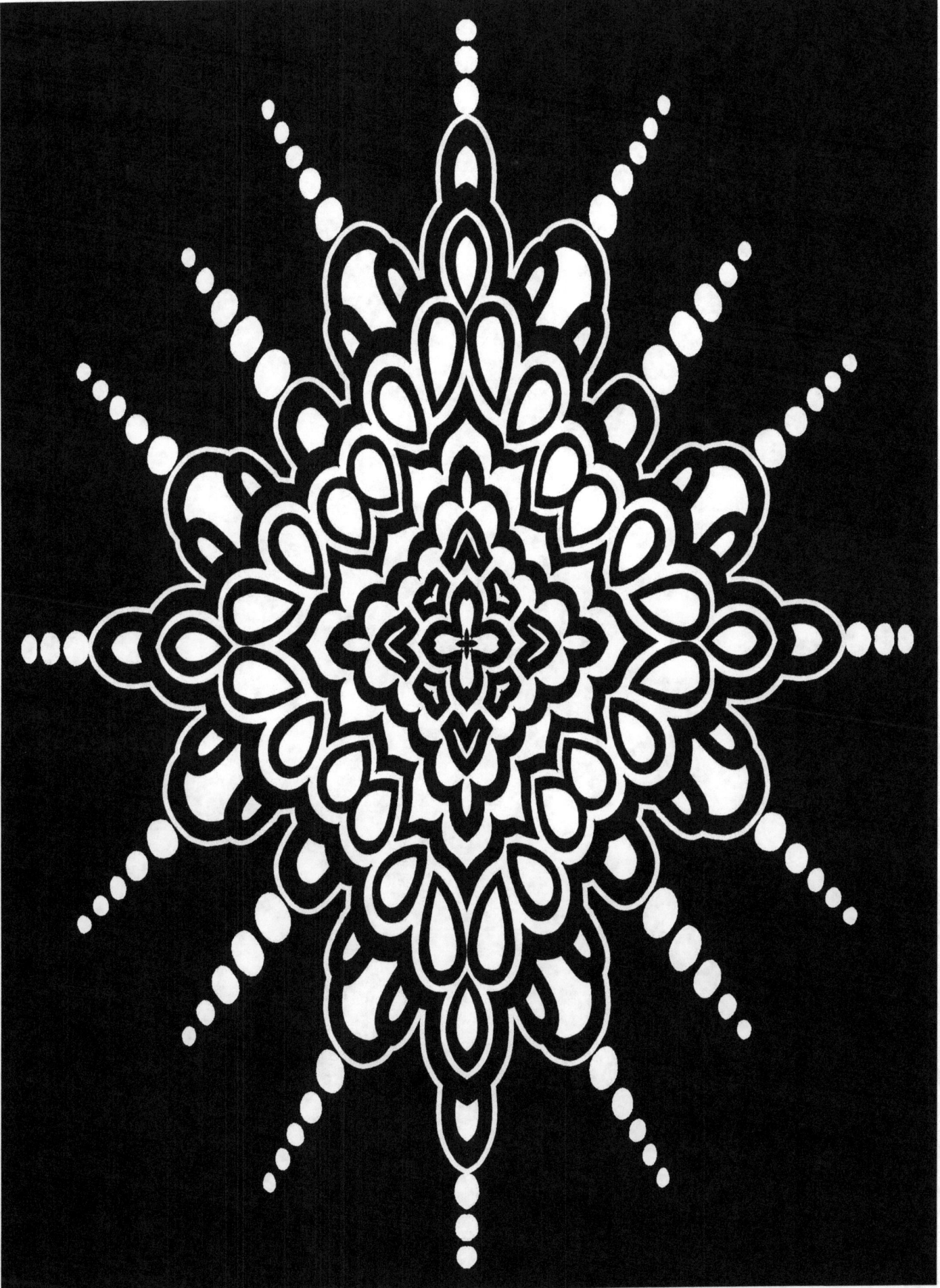

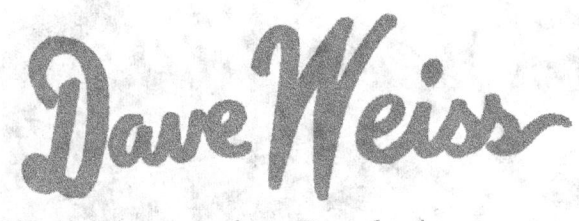

Kaleidoscopics Book 4
"Radiate"

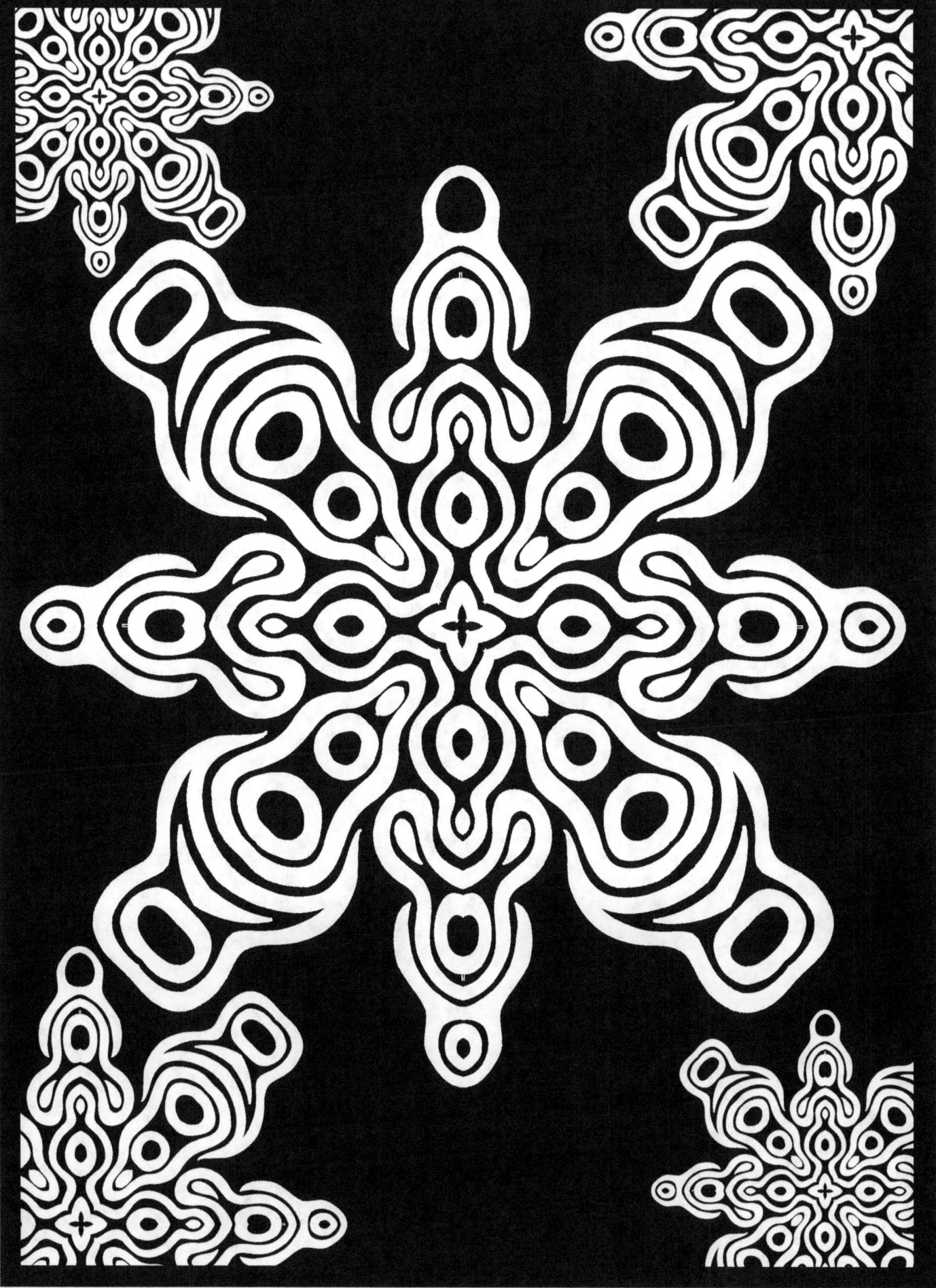

Dave Weiss

Kaleidoscopics Book 4
"Nanook"

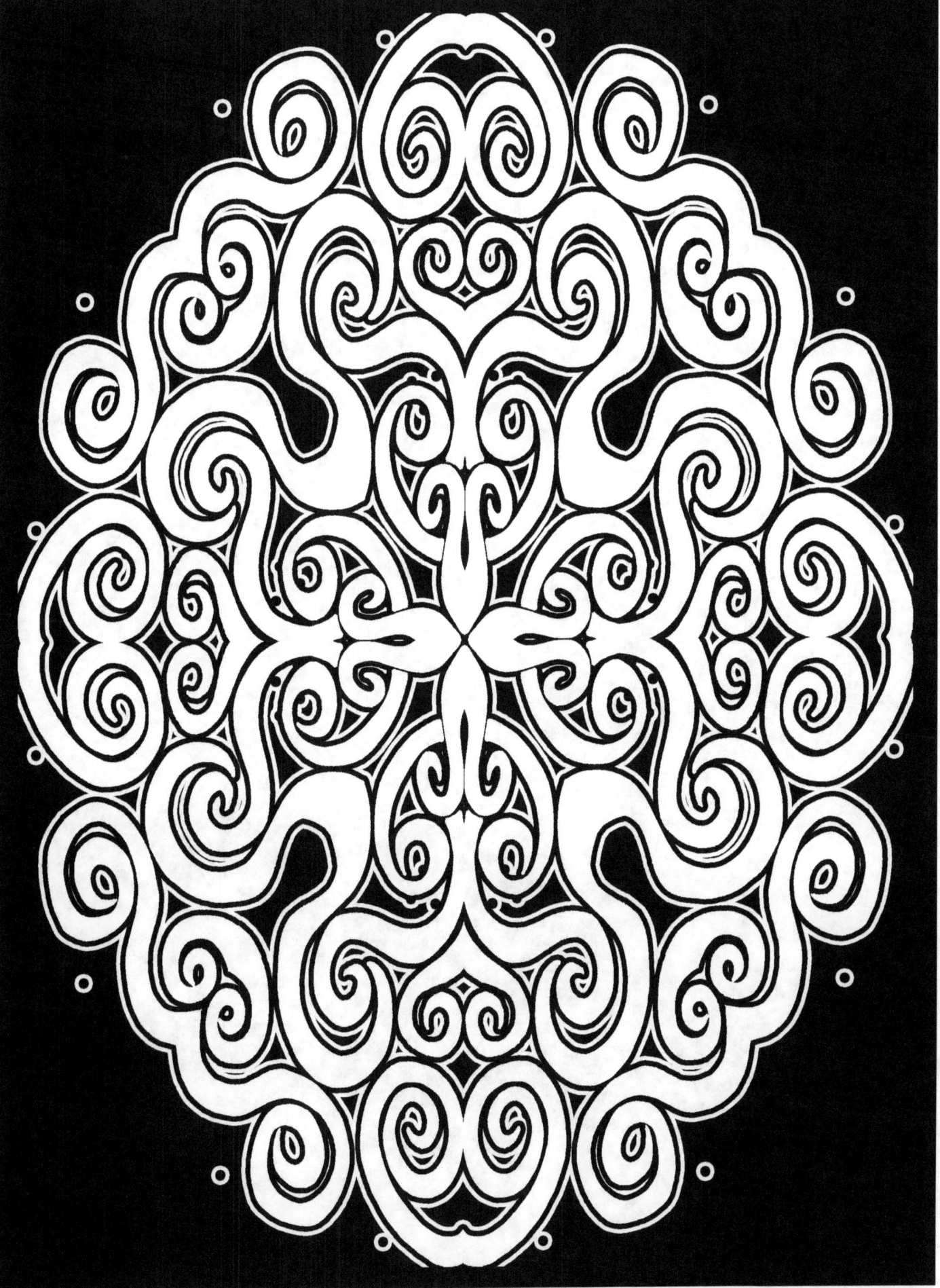

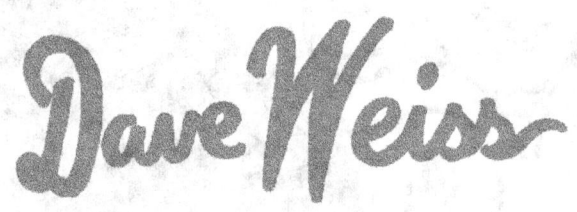

Kaleidoscopics Book 4
"Swirled and Whirled"

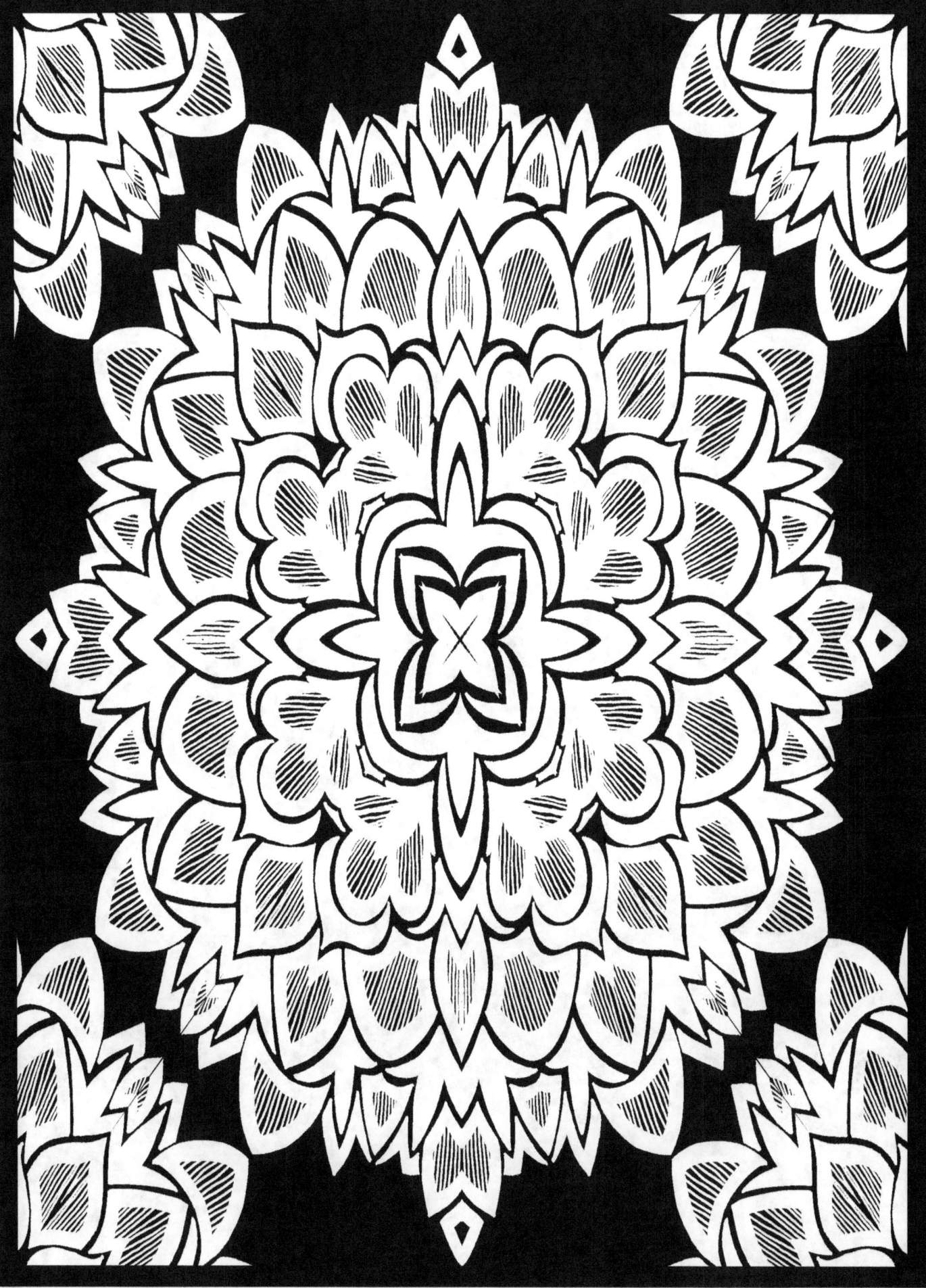

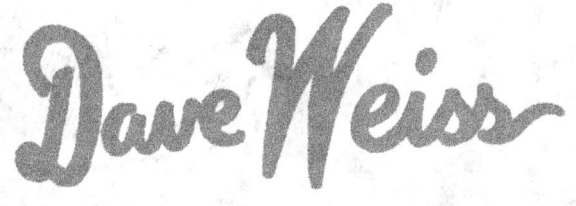

Kaleidoscopics Book 4
"Gracefully"

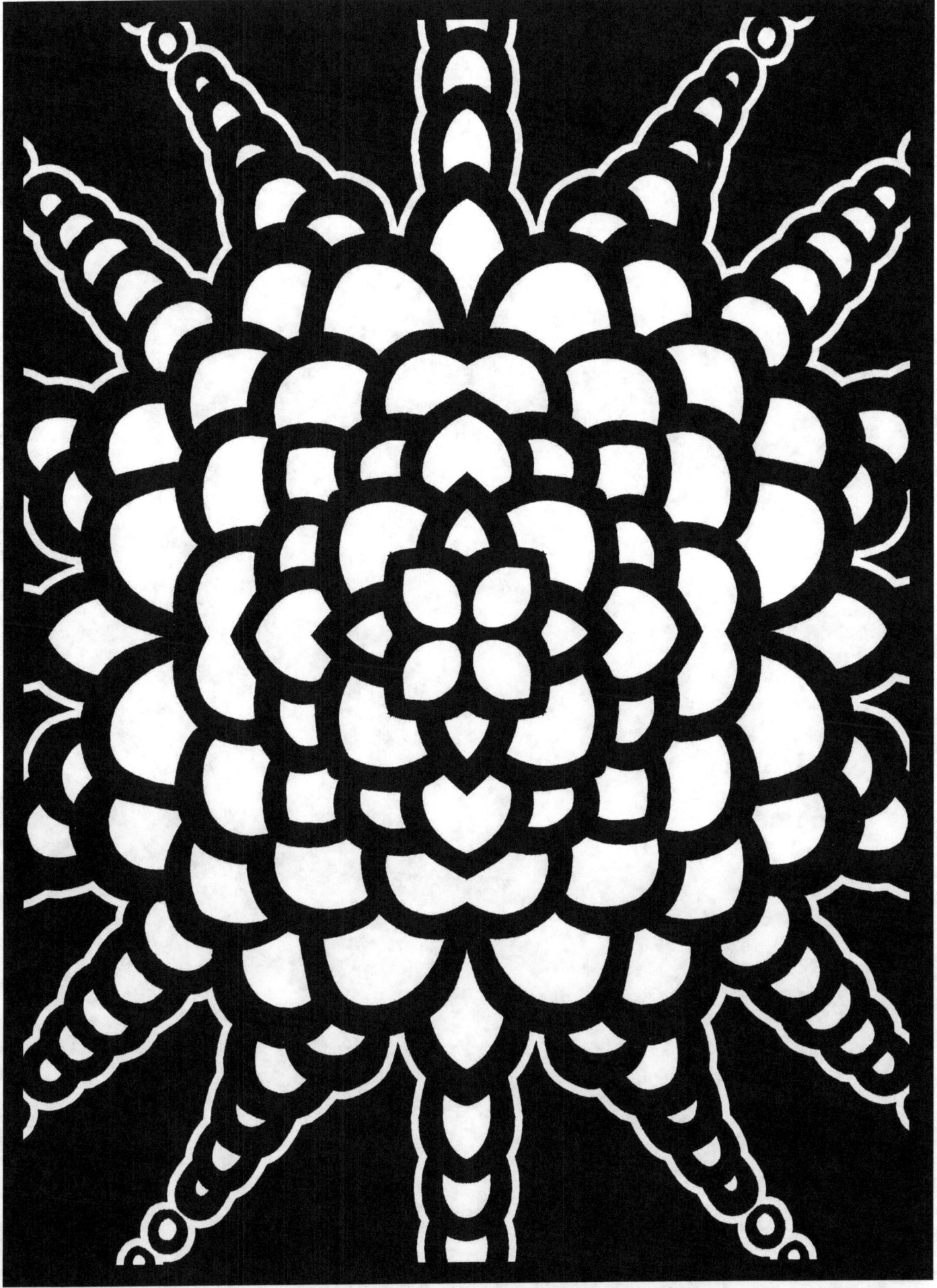

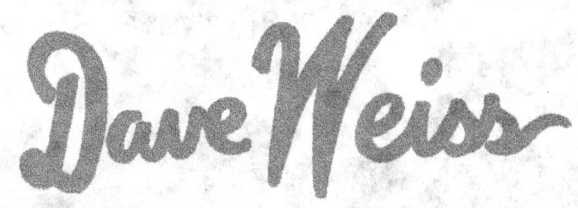

Kaleidoscopics Book 4
"Inward-Outward"

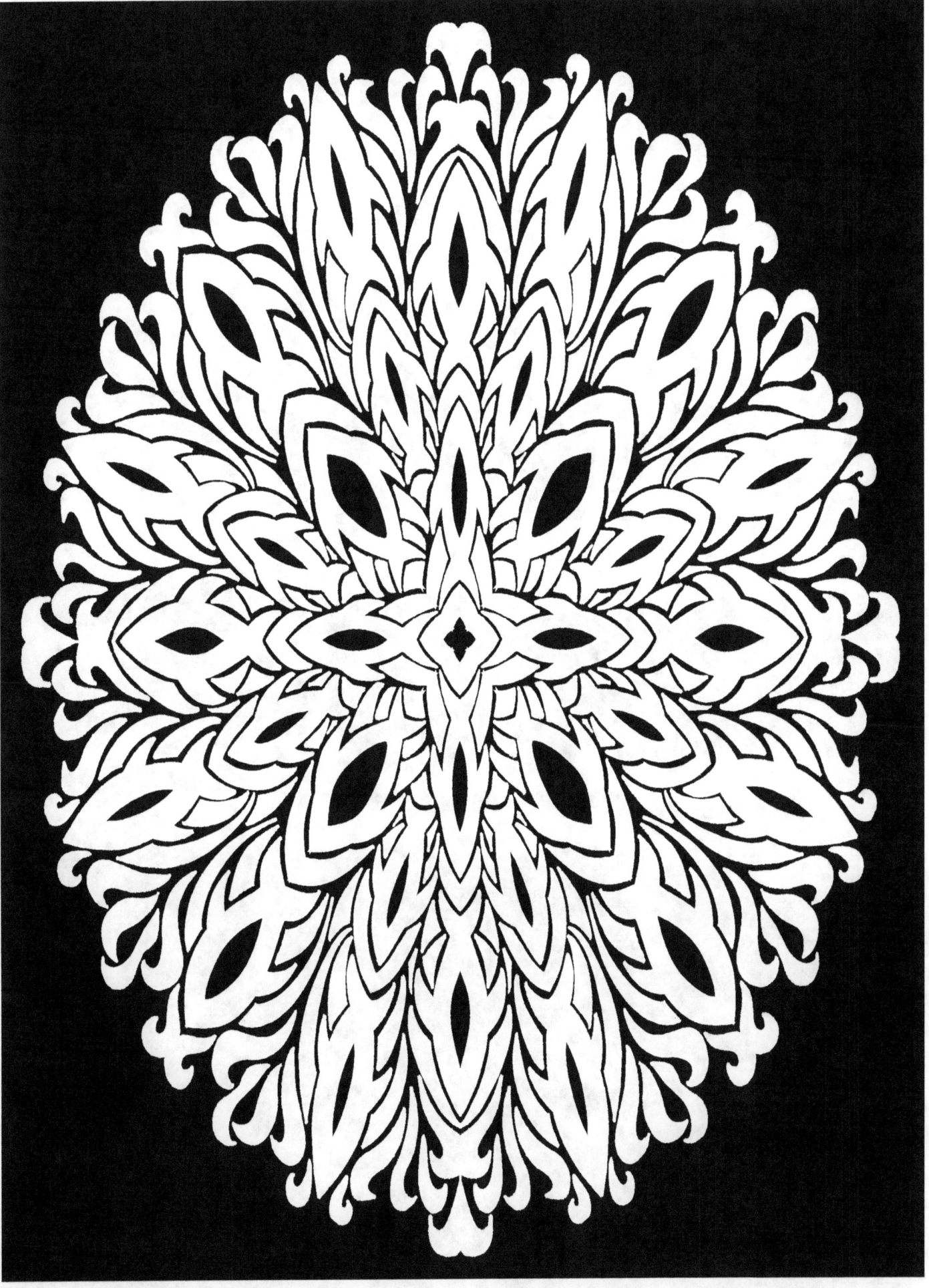

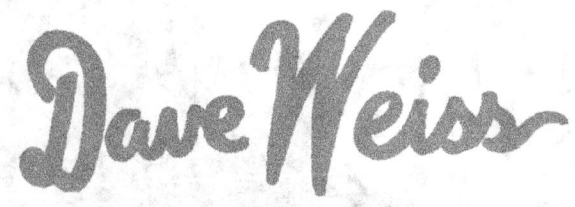

Kaleidoscopics Book 4
"Eye Pod"

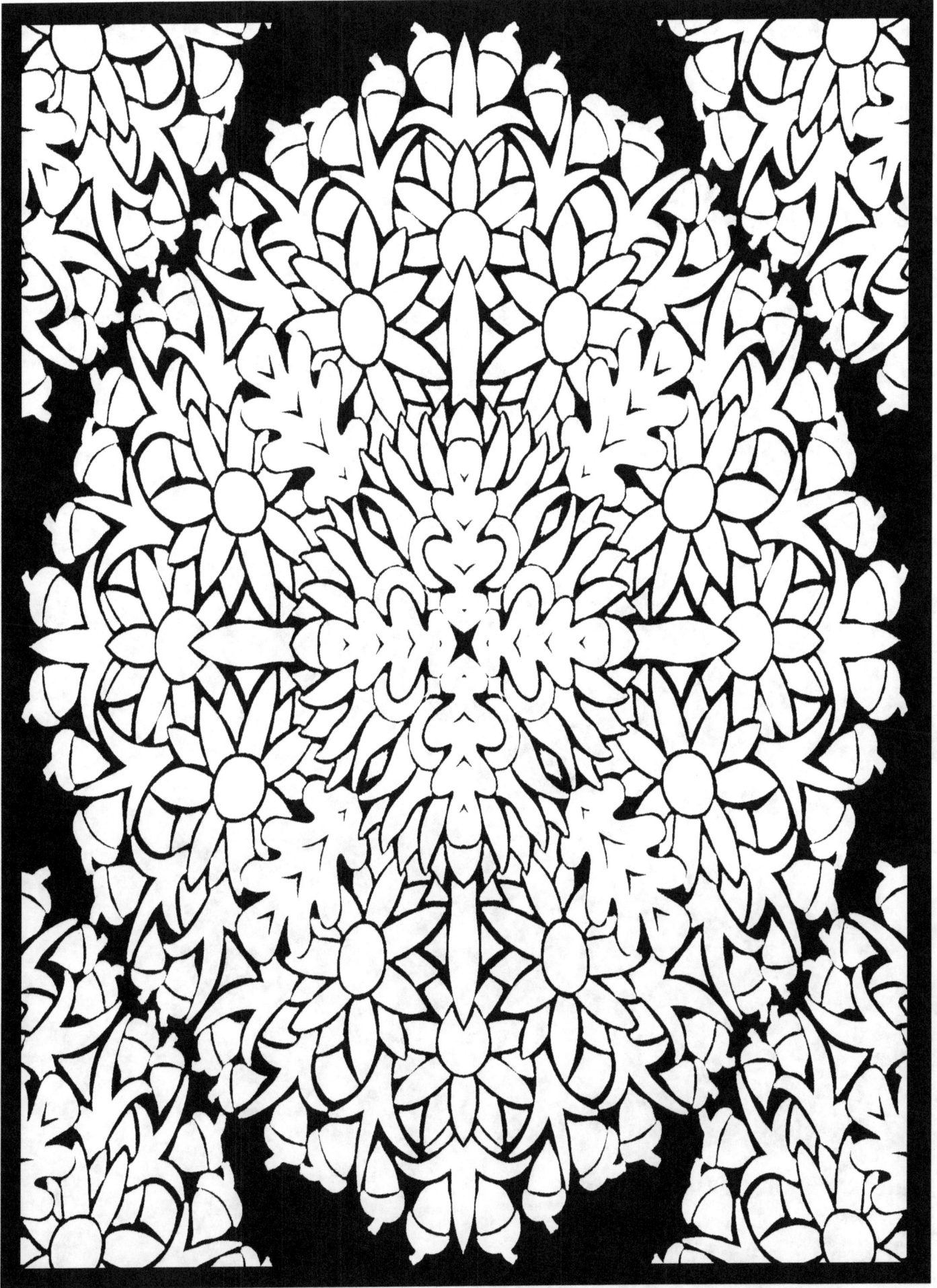

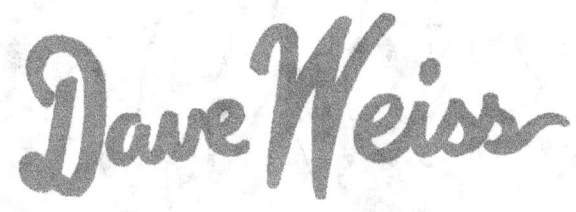

Kaleidoscopics Book 4
"Under the Old Oak Tree"

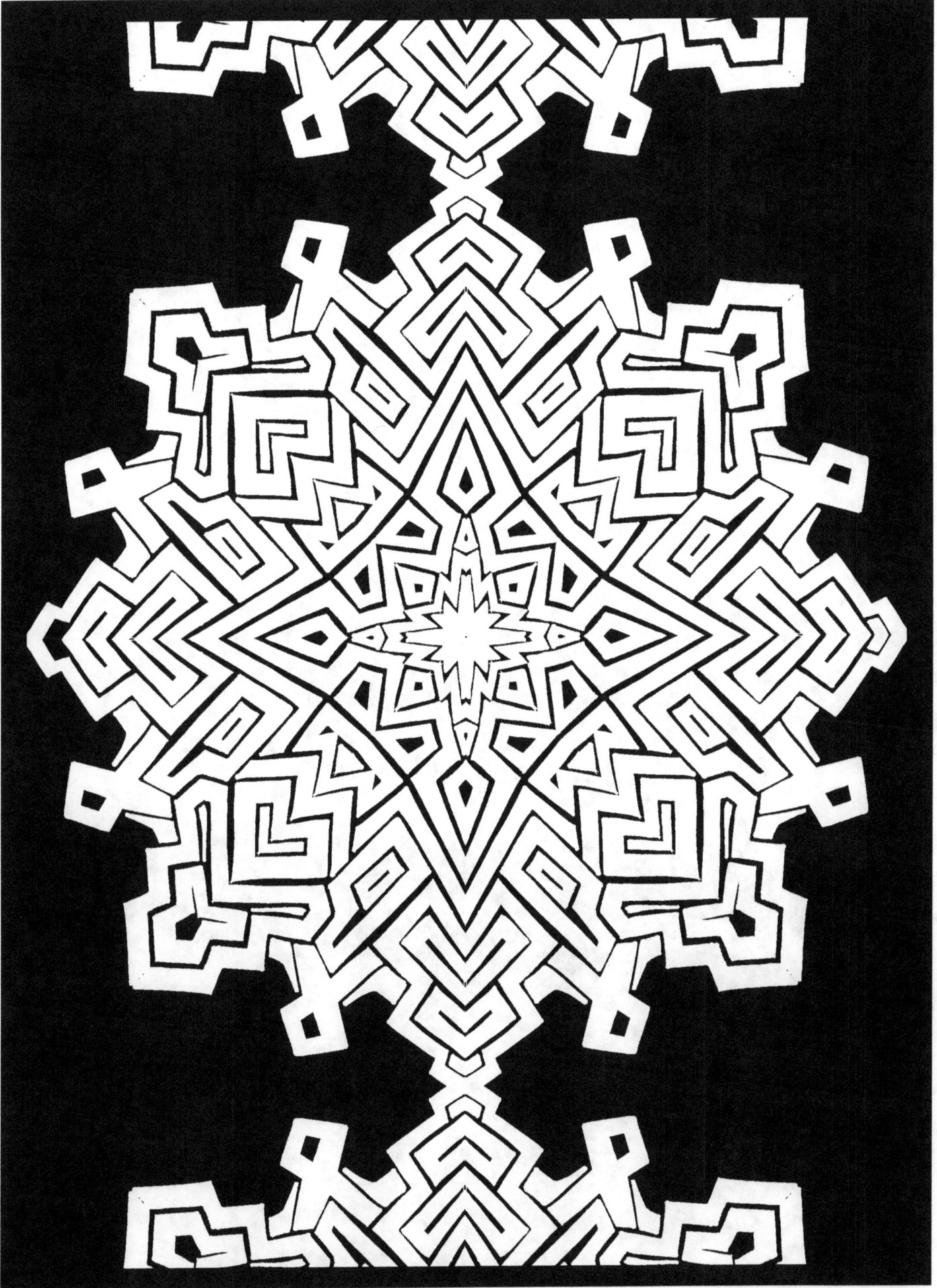

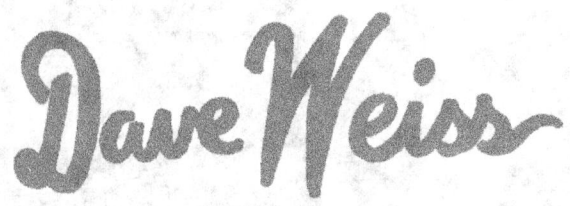

Kaleidoscopics Book 4
"That's Not Yours, It's
Mayan!"

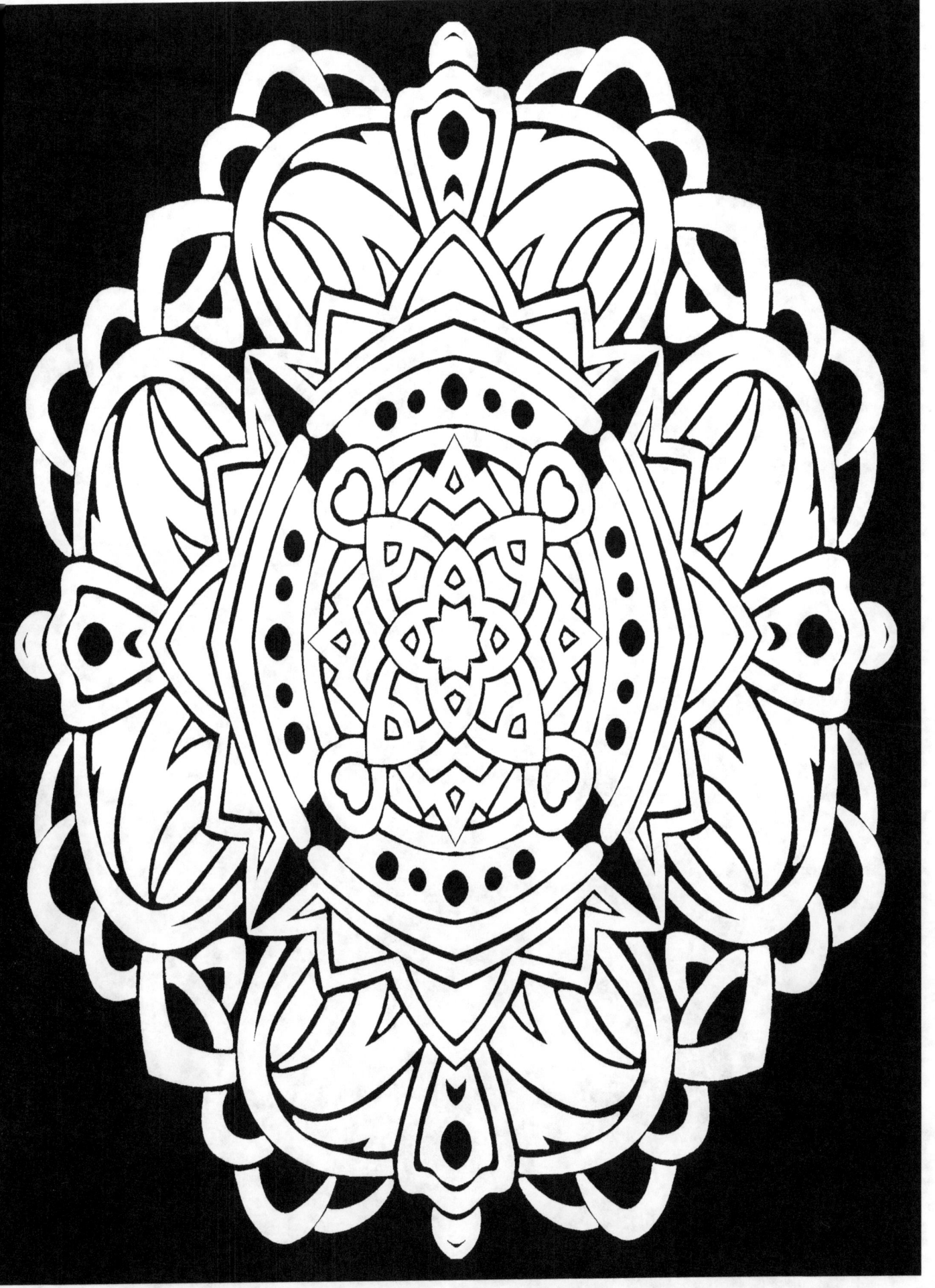

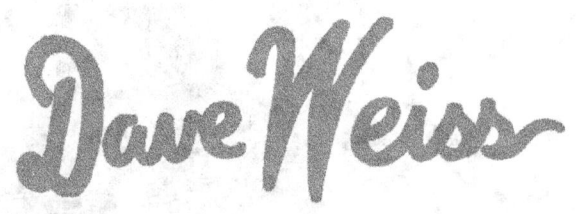

Kaleidoscopics Book 4
"Crowning Achievement"

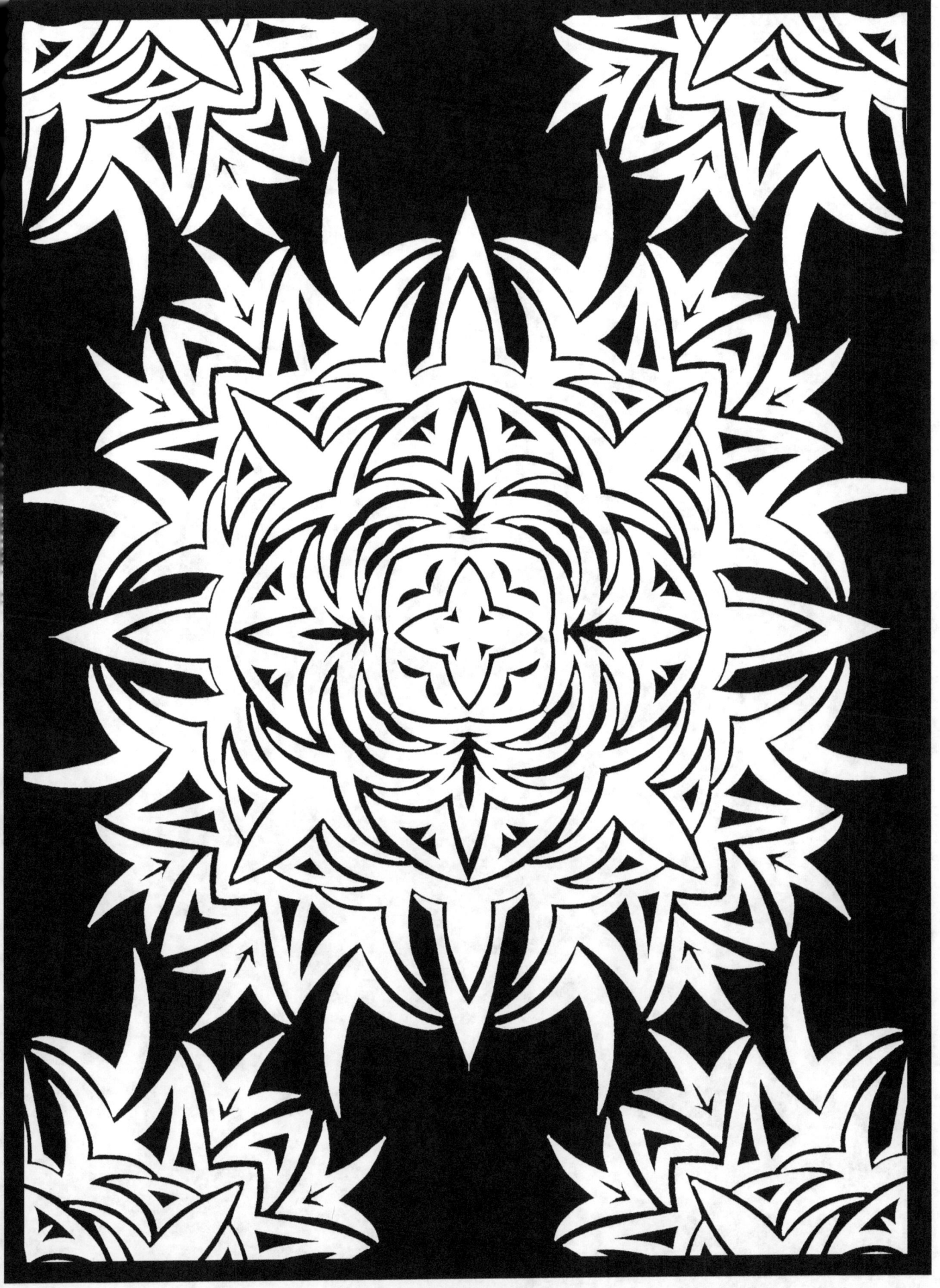

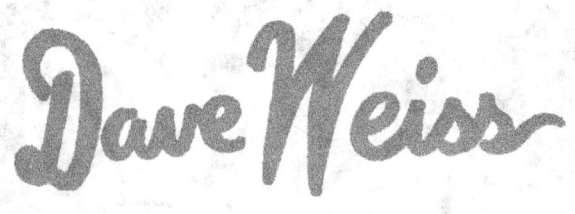

Kaleidoscopics Book 4
"Thistlism"

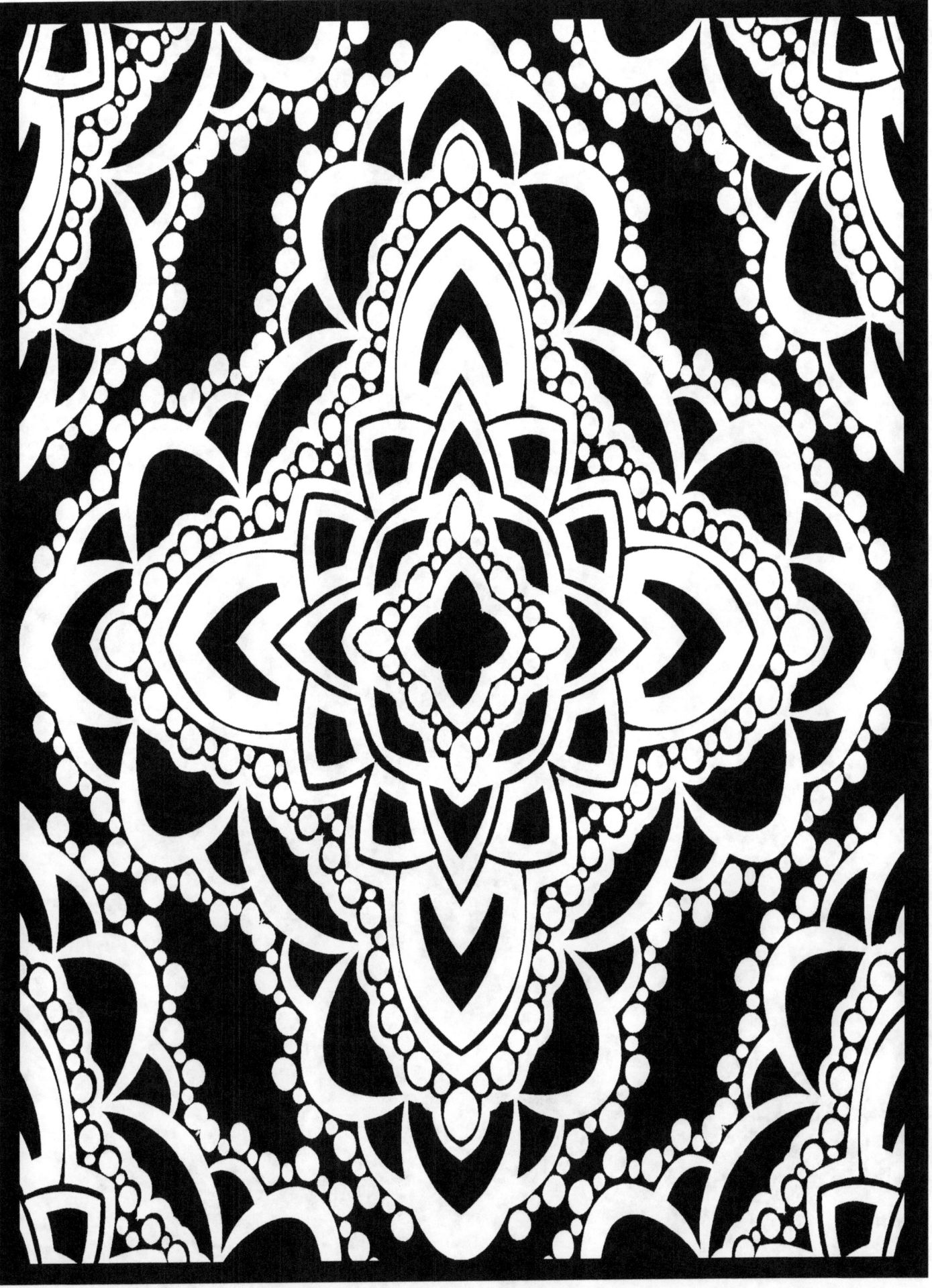

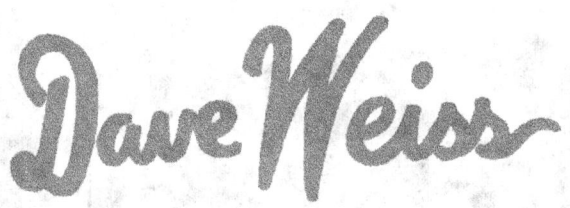

Kaleidoscopics Book 4
"Beads Me"

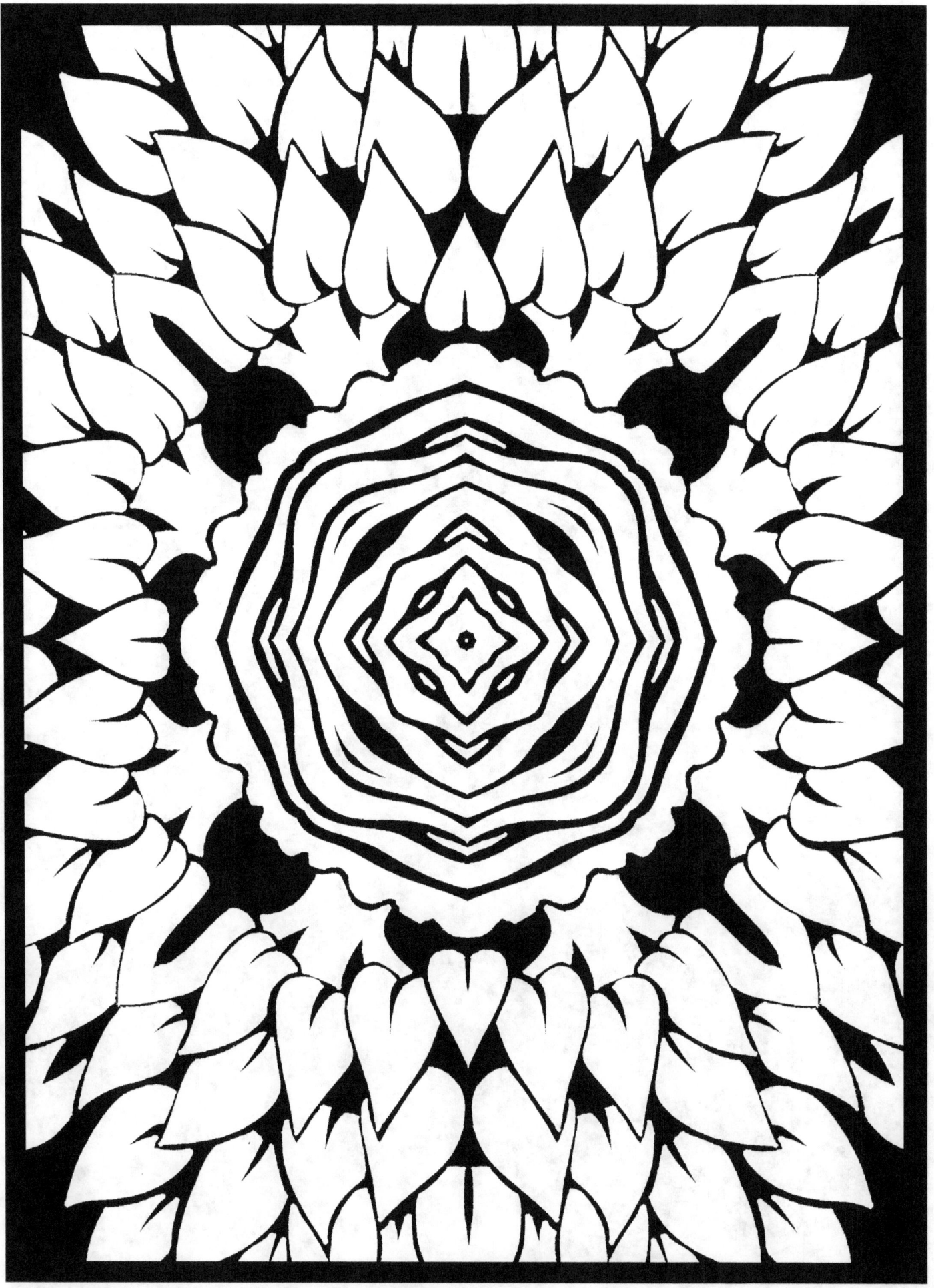

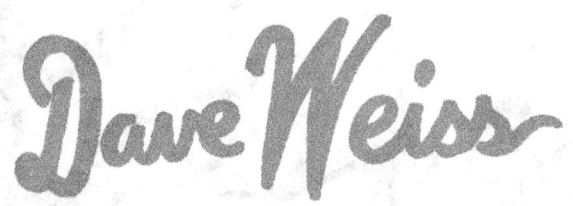

Kaleidoscopics Book 4
"Cross Section"

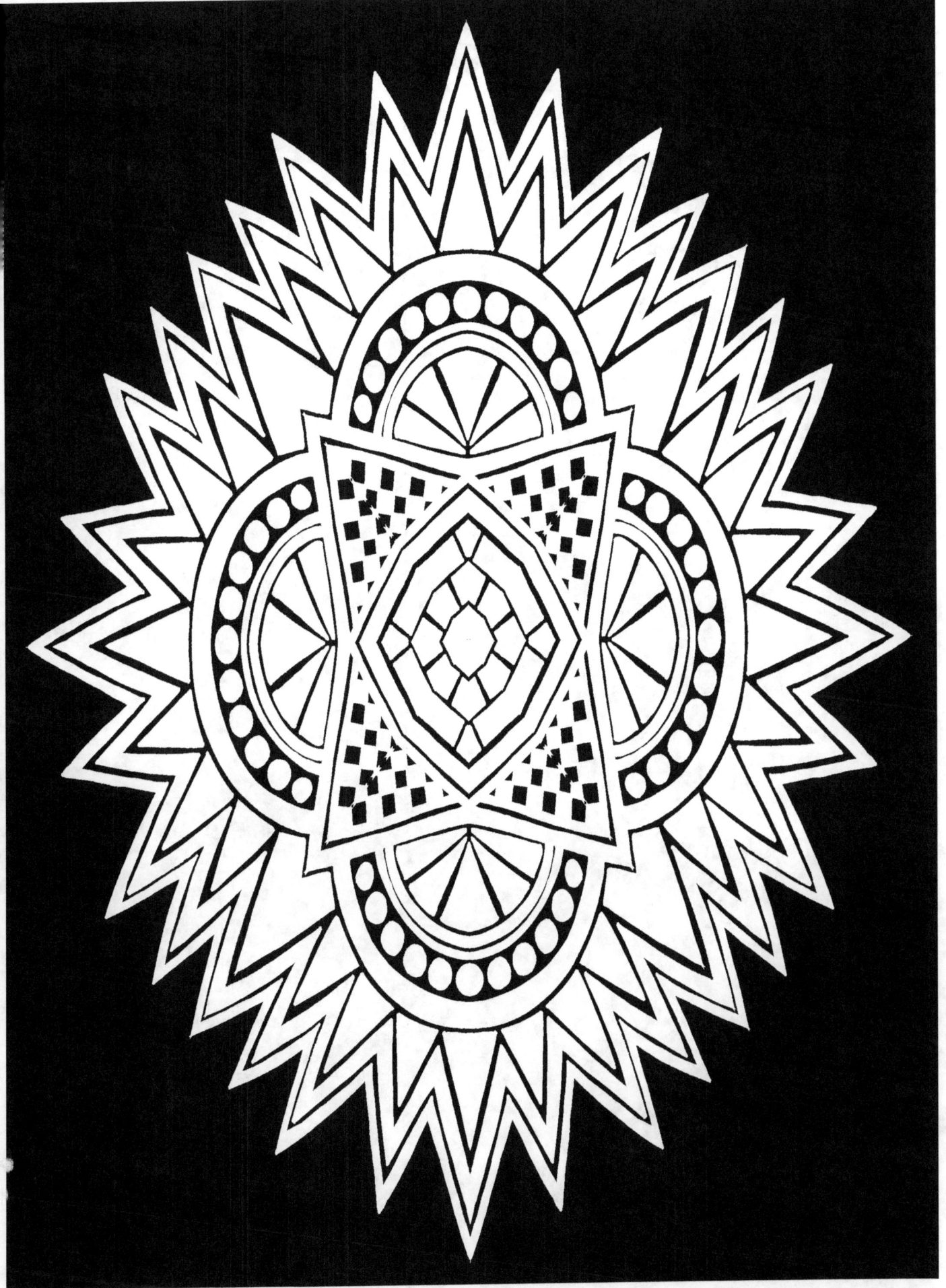

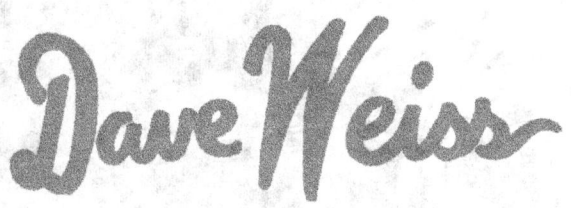

Kaleidoscopics Book 4
"Deco Disruption"

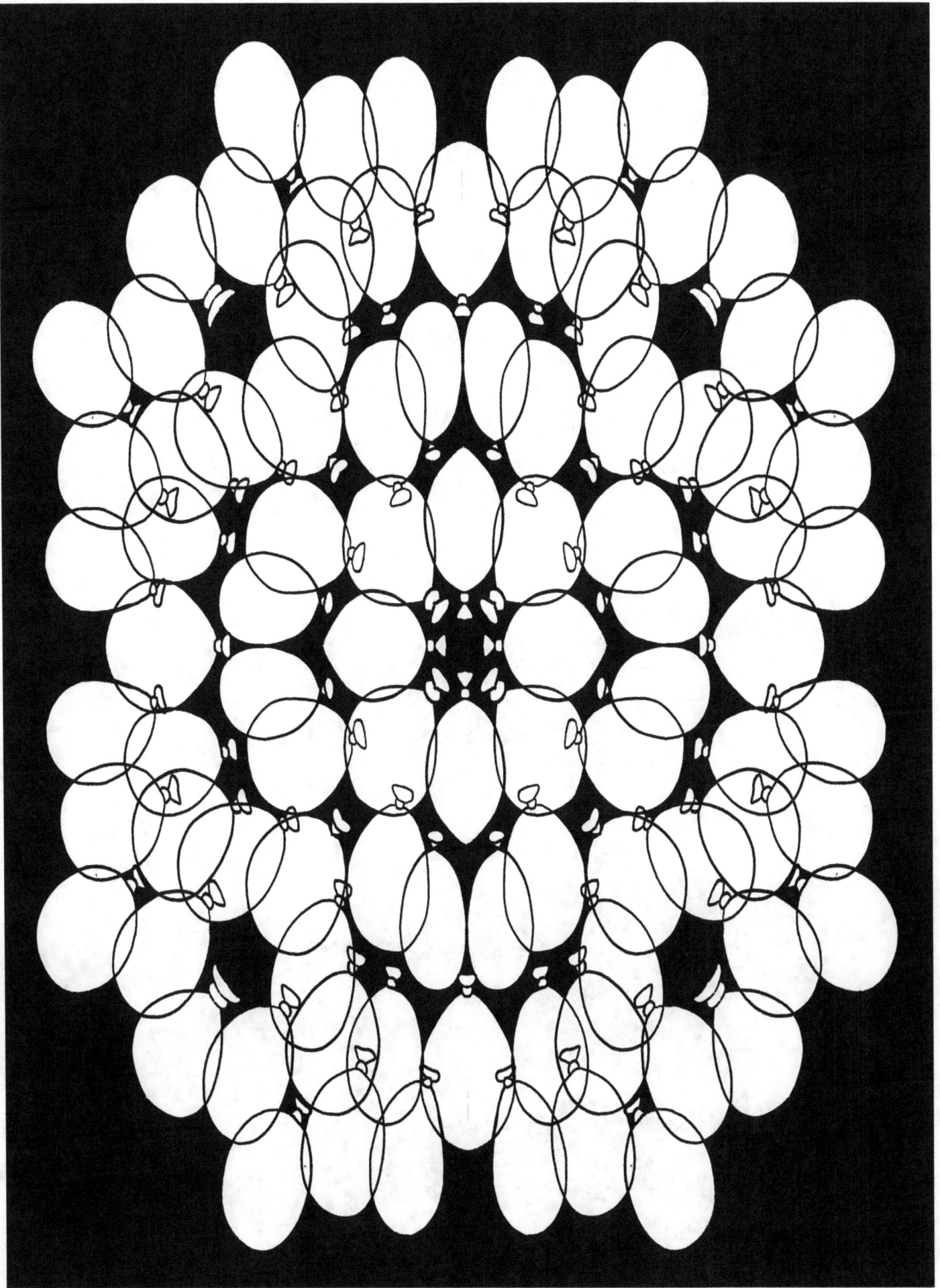

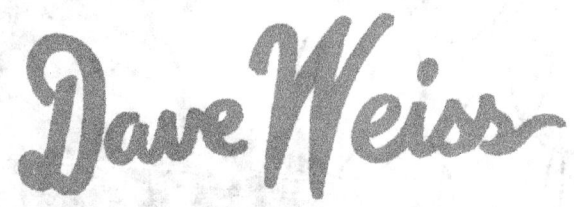

Kaleidoscopics Book 4
"Neun Und Neunzig"

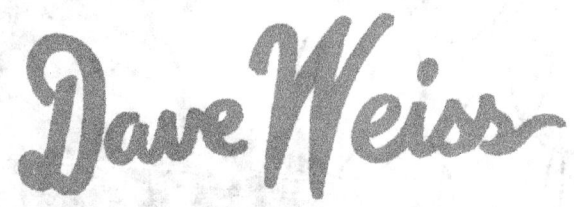

Kaleidoscopics Book 4
"Neun Und Neunzig"

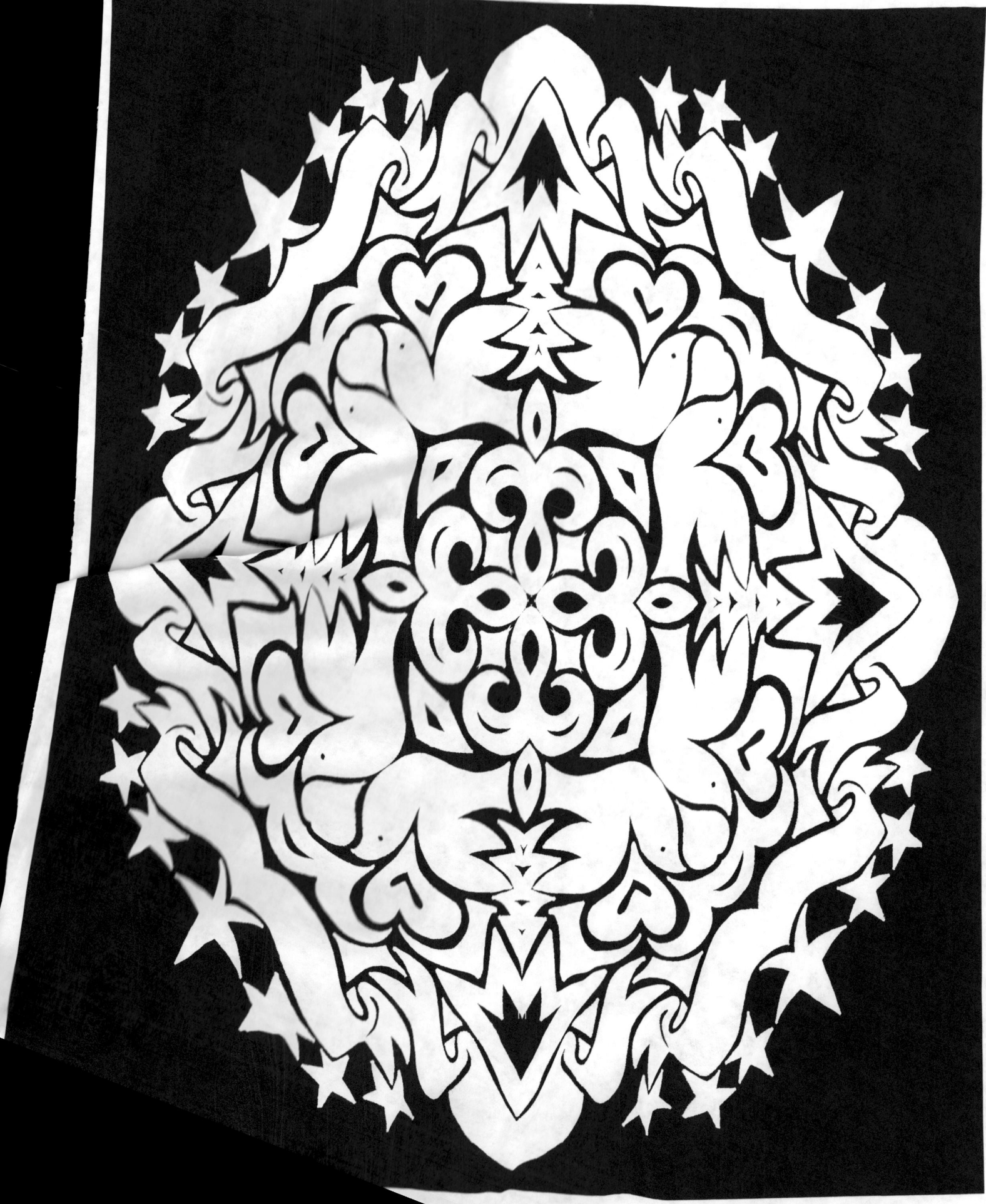

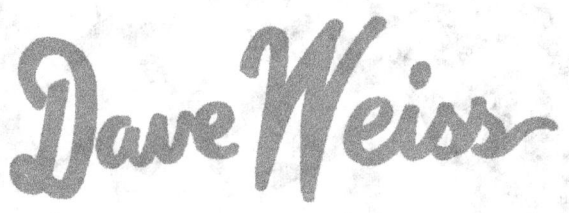

Kaleidoscopics Book 4
"Quadrangle"

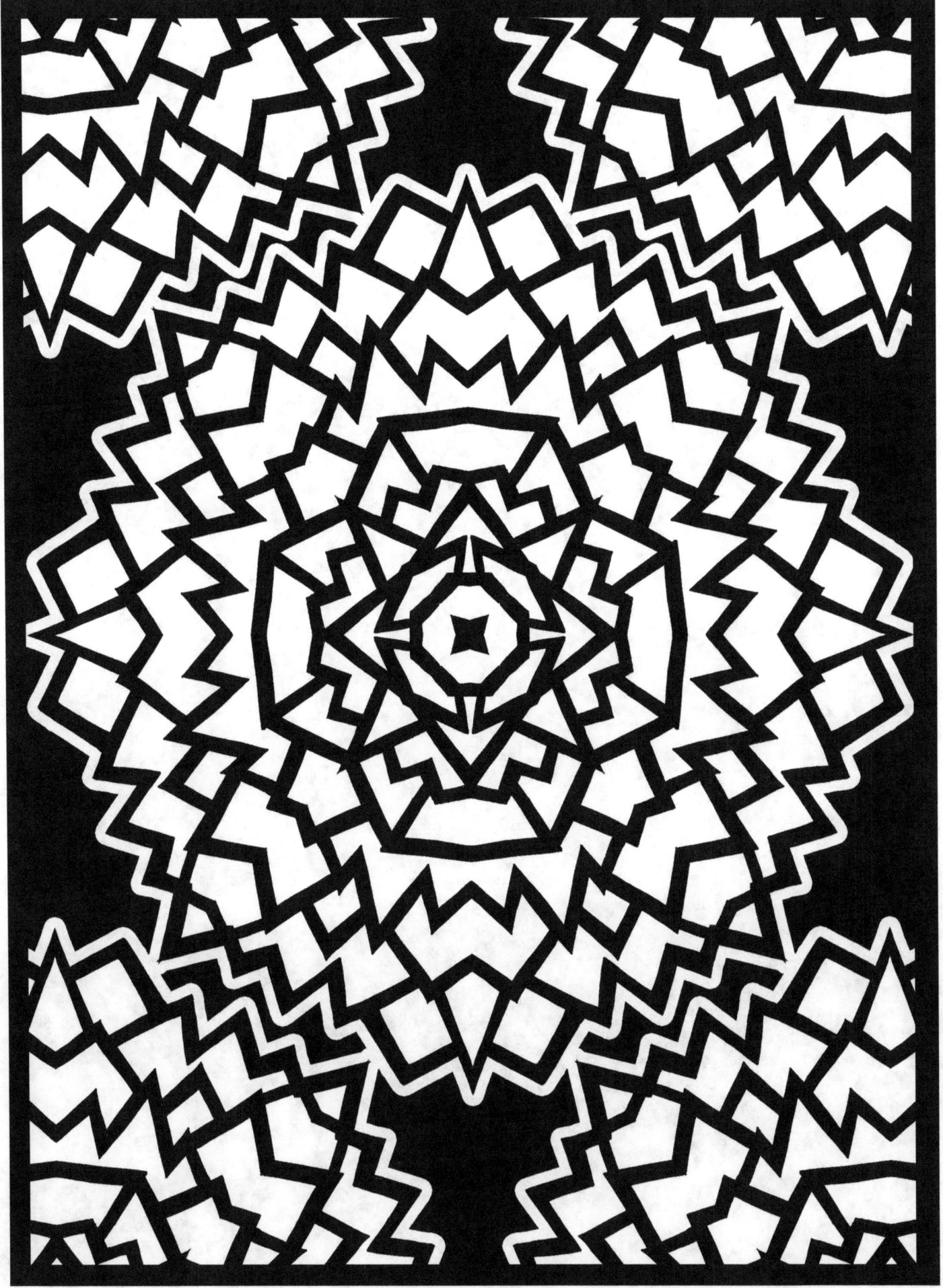

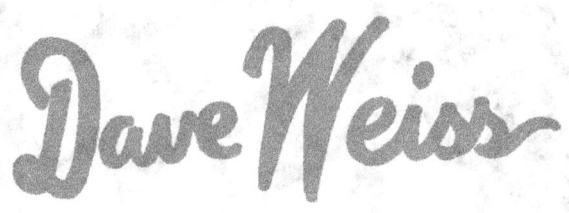

Kaleidoscopics Book 4
"Quadrangle"

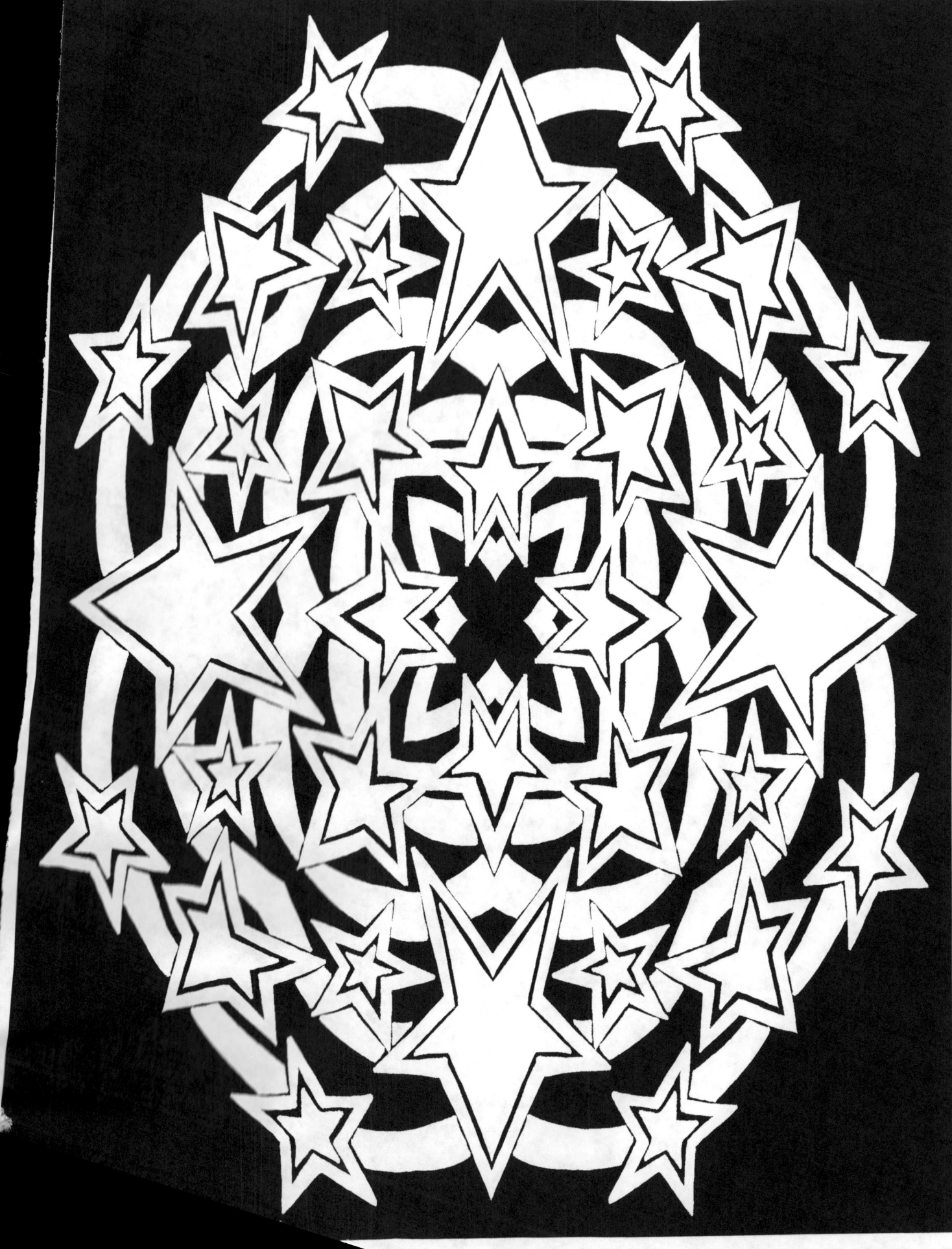